mach 1

ART OF THE Mustang

PHOTOGRAPHY BY TOM LOESER
TEXT BY DONALD FARR

motorbooks

CONTENTS

INTRODUCTION

IT STARTED WITH A SKETCH.

In 1962, Gale Halderman was a stylist assigned to the Ford design studios when his boss, Joe Oros, requested a sketch for a new, low-cost, sporty car proposed by Ford Division general manager Lee Iacocca. Busy with the 1965 Galaxie redesign, Halderman finally penciled five or six sketches to meet Oros' 8:00 a.m. deadline the next morning at 11 p.m. the night before. One of Halderman's drawings, a driver's side profile with long hood, short deck proportions and sculpturing to imply a rear quarter panel air scoop, was selected as the design that would be molded into a full-size clay model for Iacocca's approval.

During a August 16, 1962, competition between Ford's three design studios, Iacocca was immediately drawn to Halderman's design, which had been finished with a wide-mouth, Italian-looking nose and a rear end, also by Halderman, with triple-lens taillights. "The clay model looked like it was moving!" Iacocca recalled in his autobiography.

Twenty months later, the production 1965 Mustang, appearing nearly identical to Halderman's original sketch, arrived in Ford dealerships and set off near hysteria as salesmen wrote orders for 22,000 units during the first three days on-sale, a trend that would continue as the Mustang went down as one of the most successful vehicle launches in history.

It's interesting that the Mustang was conceived as a sketch, a piece of artwork. The basic shape, initially put on paper by Halderman's pencil, has survived mostly intact

for over 50 years. Although some of the iconic cues—wide-mouth grille opening, side sculpturing, tri-lens taillights, even the running horse logo—have come and gone over the years, the long hood, short rear deck look survives to this day in the latest 2015 Mustang.

Early on, Ford advertising described the Mustang as "The Car to be Made by You" to highlight the three body styles—hardtop, convertible, and fastback—and wide range of options, from stylish wheels to Décor Interior with embossed running horses in the seat backs. For the past five decades, Mustang owners have expanded that personalization concept into Mustang street machines, road racers, drag cars, restomods, and rat rods. At the other extreme, purists around the world revitalize derelict old Mustangs into immaculate restorations that look like they just rolled off the Ford assembly line. Restored or restomod, their canvas is Mustang.

For this book, *Art of the Mustang*, photographer Tom Loeser has applied his "light painting" technique to a variety of Mustangs, from concours originals to drag cars and tattered survivors, each one a piece of art in its own right. The multidimensional results allow us to see Mustangs in a new light, emphasizing the shapes, lines, and angles that have made Mustangs so appealing for over 50 years.

Even Lee Iacocca said, "We saw ourselves as artists, about to produce the finest masterpieces the world had ever seen."

1964-½-1968

THE EARLY MUSTANGS

LEE IACOCCA KNEW his job was on the line when he suggested a new, sporty car to Ford Motor Company president Henry Ford II in 1961. Still smarting from the embarrassing Edsel failure just a few years earlier, Henry II ignored Iacocca's hunch that the emerging baby boomer generation would yearn for a sportier car than Ford's stodgy early 1960s' offerings. Undeterred, Iacocca eventually gained Henry's approval by proposing his new car based on the stodgiest Ford of all—the Falcon—to hold down engineering investment costs. Henry finally gave in to Iacocca's idea, but with one caveat: "You've got to sell it." Henry II is reported as saying, "And it's your ass if you don't!"

Over the next 18 months, Iacocca's vision became the Mustang, a new automotive concept scheduled for introduction at the New York World's Fair in April 1964. Iacocca figured his job was safe if he could sell 200,000 units during the first year. But by introduction day, it was already obvious that the Mustang would be a runaway success. Ford dealers topped Iacocca's initial sales goal within a few months by delivering 250,000 Mustangs. By the car's first anniversary, sales surpassed 600,000. Before the Mustang reached its second birthday, sales reached the one million milestone.

The Mustang was more than a financial success for Ford. It was also a phenomenon that quickly became an American icon. Although based on Falcon underpinnings, the Mustang exuded sportiness with its long front end, short rear deck styling, along with standard bucket seats and floor shifter. To buyers, the Mustang was more than just a new car—it was also a statement. Driving a Mustang was the ultimate cool.

During the first four years, Ford refrained from messing with the successful Mustang formula, although new competition from Camaro, Firebird, and even corporate cousin Cougar led to a slightly larger 1967 Mustang in order to fit a 390 big-block. But the 1967–1968 model was still a Mustang with recognizable styling features—prominent grille opening with running horse emblem, side sculpturing to imply race car scoops, and triple-lens taillights. Sales continued to soar—Ford dealers sold well over two million by the end of the 1968 model year.

Carroll Shelby added to the lore with his GT350 in 1965, then the big-block GT500 in 1967. Thanks to Shelby, Mustang found success in SCCA racing, including championships in the popular Trans-Am series. With the addition of a 428 Cobra Jet option for the GT at midyear 1968, the Mustang officially joined the burgeoning muscle car scene and made the original ponycar a viable competitor on the drag strip.

In the ensuing decades, the early Mustangs became used cars, many of them disposed at salvage yards after their useful life was over. Some were reborn as drag cars, Saturday night dirt trackers, and street machines. A few were tucked away in barns to await future discovery by excited collectors.

Today, the 1965–1968 Mustangs are coveted by a worldwide legion of enthusiasts who continue to maintain, show, and race them. It's still cool to drive a Mustang.

1

1964-½ HARDTOP

TO LEE IACOCCA, the outline of the 1965 Mustang hardtop was art. His favorite angle was the side profile that provided what he called "the Mona Lisa look." It was utilized over and over in Ford's early Mustang advertising—a white hardtop against a black background to show off the new pony car's sexy long hood and short rear deck proportions.

Two men deserve much of the credit for creating the look that Iacocca pictured in his mind for a brand-new sporty car to appeal to the emerging baby-boom generation. Chief Ford stylist Joe Oros was out of town for a weeklong seminar when he learned that Iacocca had requested a design competition between Ford's three styling departments—Ford, Lincoln-Mercury, and Advanced Projects. Upon his return, Oros gathered his Ford design team, which included Gale Halderman, to discuss the design goals for Iacocca's new car. "I asked them to give consideration to three design elements," Oros recalls. "Number one was a Ferrari-type mouthy air intake and a Maserati-like die-cast center motif for the grille. Number two was that we give serious thought to having an air intake just forward of the rear axle that might direct air to the rear brakes. And three was to have consideration for a personal Thunderbird-like greenhouse in a sporty four-seater configuration."

Halderman was preparing to work late one night, on deadline for a redesign of the 1965 Galaxie, when Oros requested sketches of the new small car. He needed them by 8:00 a.m. the next morning. Halderman continued his Galaxie duty at the studio until 11:00 p.m., then headed home to focus on Oros' assignment. The following morning, Oros selected Halderman's late-night drawing as one of the designs that would be molded in clay for Iacocca's design competition. Halderman's styling incorporated the long hood, short rear deck profile preferred by Iacocca, who admittedly admired the look of Lincoln's 1956 Continental Mark II. As someone else explained, "A long hood indicates there's a lot of engine under there."

Halderman's sketch also incorporated side sculpturing that simulated rear-brake cooling scoops and taillights with three-element lenses. Both were incorporated into the clay model that was displayed, along with five models from the other styling departments, for Iacocca's review on August 16, 1962. "When he saw our finished car, he just rolled his cigar in his mouth," Halderman told Jim Smart during a *Mustang Monthly* interview. "I could see the gleam in his eye; he was pleased as punch."

The clay model made from Halderman's sketch was later approved by Henry Ford II, and the Mustang was on its way to production with a projected introduction at the New York World's Fair in April 1964.

Other than the optional wire wheelcovers, Paul Segura's Wimbledon White 1964 1/2 hardtop is identical to the "Mona Lisa look" Mustang that was used in much of Ford's promotional material. With the base 170-cubic-inch six-cylinder and three-speed automatic, Paul's hardtop was one of thousands sold at or near "$2,368 F.O.B. Detroit," as the advertising copy touted. The Mustang and its advertising campaign rank among the most successful in automotive history, with Ford dealers selling nearly 700,000 units during the 1965 Mustang's extended 16-month production cycle. Mustang sales would top one million in February 1966, less than two years after its introduction.

Paul's hardtop was built on July 30, 1964, just two weeks before Ford switched to 1965 production. Although Mustangs built between March 9 and mid-August, 1964, have become identified as 1964 1/2 models, all were actually titled as 1965s. Due to the Mustang's early introduction, some five months before the usual September new-car intros, the early Mustangs were assembled during Ford's 1964 production cycle and therefore have a number of 1964 characteristics, primarily components related to the generator charging system, which was updated to a more efficient alternator system for 1965.

Paul bought his hardtop from the original owner in 1983, paying $600 for what Paul describes as a "basket case." Over the next two years, Paul restored the Mustang himself except for the engine rebuild. For the past 30 years, Paul has been steadily making improvements in a process that he describes as "ongoing."

2

1965 GT350
SCHOOL CAR

BEFORE THE COBRA, and a couple of years before the Shelby GT350 Mustang, Carroll Shelby opened a driving school at the old Riverside International Raceway in southern California. His driving career over due to a heart condition, 37-year-old Shelby wanted to keep his fingers in the racing business. Recalling his early competition days, when he could have used some basic driving instruction himself, Shelby began developing an idea for what would become the Carroll Shelby School of High Performance Driving, which opened in early 1961 for up-and-coming race car drivers.

A young Peter Brock was in the right place at the right time when Shelby needed someone to run the school. For students who didn't have their own cars, Brock initially utilized a bug-eye Sprite and an open-wheel BMC Formula Junior, but they were soon replaced by cars from Shelby's "other" project, the Cobra sports car. While testing Cobras or riding along with Shelby development driver Ken Miles, Brock established the school's first curriculum, which taught the basics of driver position, apex and turning points, braking points, drifting, and car control. Sessions spanned five days for $500, or $1,000 for students who used the school cars.

When it opened, the Carroll Shelby School of High Performance Driving was the only driving school in the United States. With instructors such as Bob Bondurant and John Timanus, it was soon rated as one of the top driving schools in the world.

Later, the school moved to Willow Springs International Raceway where, in 1965, a trio of Shelby Mustang GT350s—VINs 5021, 5029, and 5S451—were enlisted as the school cars. They were essentially street cars but equipped with competition upgrades from Shelby's race shop, including a four-point roll bar, larger radiator, and the R-model front valance with its improved cooling capacity for both the engine and brakes. Larger 32-gallon fuel tanks, as used in the GT350 R-models, were also added so instructors and students wouldn't have to interrupt their sessions for refueling.

According to Shelby American Automobile Club records, the second school GT350, 5S029, was completed at Shelby American's Venice, California, facility on January 8, 1965, and then shipped to Hi-Performance Motors, a dealership that was also a Carroll Shelby company, before being sold to the school. With "Carroll Shelby School of High Performance" lettered across the doors and front fenders, the early production GT350 served as a school car until Shelby turned the operation over to Bondurant, who reopened it as the Bondurant School of High Performance Driving in February 1968. Now located in Phoenix, the Bondurant school continues to operate today.

Like all 1965 GT350s, 5029 was powered by a 306-horsepower Cobra version of the 289 High Performance small-block. Shelby American also modified the fastback with the usual GT350 performance upgrades: fiberglass hood with scoop, Koni shocks, lowered front A-arms, rear traction bars, dash pod with 8,000-rpm tachometer and oil pressure gauge, competition seat belts, and a fiberglass rear shelf that replaced the rear seat, which effectively made the GT350 a two-seater and legal for SCCA racing.

When Bruce Kawaguchi acquired 5029 in 1974 from its second owner, it was just an old Shelby that was missing its drivetrain, hood, fenders, and interior. However, the roll bar and 32-gallon fuel tank were still in place, along with the number 77 painted on an oval background on the doors. When Bruce started sanding off the race numbers, he discovered blue "High Perf . . ." lettering underneath. "I recognized it from photos in an old *Car & Driver*," Bruce says. Later, he was able to confirm the car's history at Shelby's driving school.

A restoration was started in 2001 but not completed until 2010, just in time for an unveiling at the SAAC-35 national convention at Infineon Raceway. The restoration took the car back to its condition when used at the Carroll Shelby School of High Performance Driving. "I wanted it nice but not concours," Bruce adds, "because I knew I was going to put it back on the track."

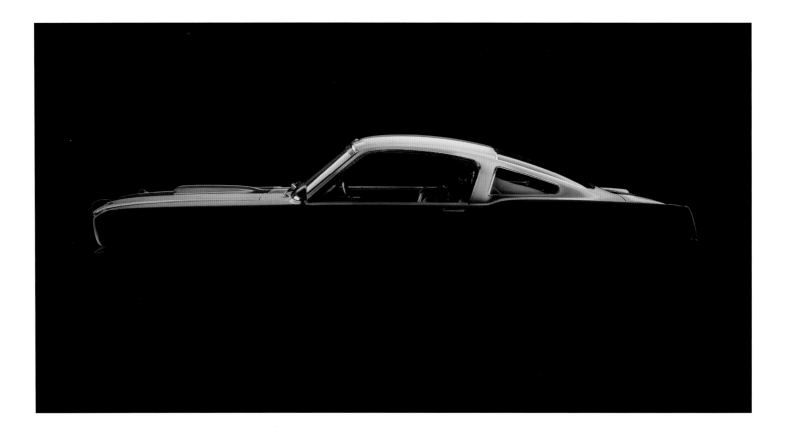

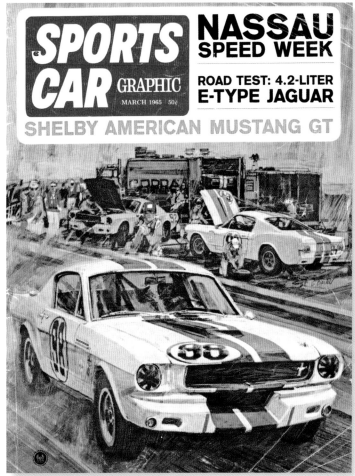

3

1965 HARDTOP 289

IT'S HARD TO SAY which is more synonymous with the other—the 289 in the Mustang or the Mustang powered by the 289.

When the 1965 Mustang was introduced on April 17, 1964, some five months before the 1965 Fords, the engine availability came from Ford's 1964 powertrain lineup: 170-cubic-inch six-cylinder, 260 two-barrel V-8, and a pair of four-barrel 289s, including the solid-lifter Hi-Po. When Ford switched to 1965 production in the fall, the older 260 was replaced by a two-barrel version of the 289, an engine displacement that would be forever linked to the first-generation 1965–1966 Mustangs.

In 1965, the 289 was the latest configuration for Ford's Windsor series of small-block engines, which had debuted in 1962 with 221 cubic inches as the replacement for the heavy, bulky, and outdated Y-block V-8. With the trend toward smaller cars such as the Fairlane and Falcon, Ford needed a lighter, more compact V-8 to power its vehicles of the future. Identified as "Windsor" because it was initially built at Ford's engine assembly plant in Windsor, Ontario, the new V-8's block was an advanced thin-wall casting, making the 221 much smaller and lighter, at 470 pounds, than its Y-block predecessor. With wedge heads and a two-barrel carburetor for 145 horsepower, the 221 was originally used in the Fairlane and Mercury Meteor.

The Windsor's displacement expansion began at mid-1962 with an increase to 260 cubic inches for 164 horsepower, a boost needed to power full-size Fords. The 260 was later employed for the Fairlane, the Falcon, and eventually the new 1965 Mustang.

The Windsor reached its most well-known displacement in 1963 when the piston bores were enlarged for 289 cubic inches. In both two-barrel and four-barrel form, the 289 found its way into most Fords, including optionally in the 1964 1/2 Mustang, with an Autolite four-barrel carburetor for 210 horsepower. During 1965 and 1966, the 289 was available in the Mustang as a two-barrel with 200 horsepower, a four-barrel with 225 horsepower, and a solid-lifter 289 High Performance with a high-revving 271 ponies.

New luxury interiors, new GT performance package for America's favorite sports car

The 289 in Paul Segura's Honey Gold 1965 hardtop is the base two-barrel version, which powered the majority of V-8 Mustangs during 1965 and 1966. Identified as the "C-code" due to its fifth-digit letter in the Vehicle Identification Number, Paul's 289 is equipped with the power steering pump and air conditioning compressor, all immaculately restored to Mustang Club of America concours standards. In 1965, Ford was still using a variety of paint treatments to identify its engines, so Paul's 289 is painted factory-correct with a black short-block trimmed with gold air cleaner and valve covers.

Paul found his hardtop in Huntington Beach, California, in 1990, and he was soon tearing into the Mustang for a ground-up restoration. "I pride myself on bringing vintage Mustangs back to their original equipment and condition," says Paul, who is an assistant head judge for the Mustang Owners Club of California. "Everything on this car is original, right down to the brake cylinders."

Paul's Mustang was well-optioned from the factory with power steering and brakes, a short console to clear the factory hang-on air conditioning, wire wheel covers, Visibility Group, emergency flashers, and back-up lamps. Mustangs with the two-barrel 289 were normally equipped with a single muffler and exhaust system, but Paul's was ordered with the optional dual exhaust.

Interestingly, the hardtop was built at Ford's San Jose, California, assembly plant, and then shipped cross-country to a Ford dealership in Jacksonville, Florida. Shortly after its purchase, the original owner moved to California, taking the Mustang cross-country with him. It's been a California car ever since, as proven by its vintage blue and yellow California license plate.

The 289 was a mainstay Mustang powerplant through 1968, when it was replaced by a 302-cubic-inch version of the Windsor. With the exception of 1974, a Windsor-based engine was available for the Mustang from 1965 to 1995, ending its three-decade run as the legendary 5.0-liter High Output.

4

1966 SHELBY GT350H

BY 1966, Ford's objective for the Shelby GT350 had changed. A year earlier, Ford president Lee Iacocca craved a racing pedigree for his new Mustang, which Shelby American emphatically delivered with the SCCA B-Production championship for the 1965 GT350. For 1966, Ford wanted to take advantage of the racing success by selling more GT350s at a greater profit per unit. That resulted in side scoops and rear quarter windows to differentiate the premium-priced Shelby from the standard Mustang fastback, along with the elimination of certain modifications, including side-exit exhaust and 1965's tachometer dash pod, to contain costs. To appeal to a wider audience, Shelby American also opened up the Mustang's color palette (1965 was white only), retained the back seat, softened the suspension, and added an automatic transmission to the option list.

No doubt those changes alone ensured that Shelby American would top 1965's 562 units. Then the Hertz Corporation, which had recently switched its rental fleet from General Motors to Ford, contacted Shelby about supplying GT350s for its Hertz Sports Car Club program. Shelby American secured the deal when sales manager Peyton Cramer delivered a black GT350 prototype with gold stripes, the color combination used to distinguish Hertz rental cars when the company was founded in 1925. Initially, Hertz ordered 200 Shelby Mustangs, renamed GT350H. Then, in an unexpected boost to Shelby American's bottom line, another order arrived for an additional 800 cars, bringing the total to 1,000. (Final production would come to 1,001, including two prototypes). The Hertz order alone nearly doubled Shelby GT350 sales over 1965.

For a period spanning late 1965 to early 1967, the 1966 Shelby GT350H Mustangs were available from Hertz rental counters for $17 a day plus 17 cents per mile. Afterwards, most of the cars were "disposed of" through Shelby American's Ford dealership chain as used cars. Today, they are coveted collector cars, not only as Shelbys but also for their unique rental car history.

Over the years, a number of myths emerged about the GT350H Shelbys. There were plenty of stories about Hertz Shelbys being used for weekend competition, then returned to Hertz on Monday morning, many of them true. Some were reportedly dropped off at Hertz with 289 two-barrel engines, the Shelby's 306-horsepower Cobraized 289 High Performance having found its way into the renter's personal Mustang.

Another fable claimed that all 1966 Hertz Shelbys were equipped with the automatic transmission, but Shelby American Automobile Club records show that the first 85 were fitted with four-speed manuals. Because the majority were painted in the Hertz black-and-gold scheme, many assumed that it was the only color combination used on the GT350H. However, Hertz also requested shades from the Mustang's standard color mix, resulting in nearly 25 percent that were not Raven Black—71 Wimbledon White, 60 Candy Apple Red, 55 Sapphire Blue, and 58 Ivy Green, all with gold GT350H side stripes.

Daniel Swana's 1966 GT350H, 6S955, was among the non-black Hertz Shelbys. Originally delivered to the Hertz fleet in Pensacola, Florida, the Candy Apple Red fastback survived its rental duty and was eventually sold to second owner Del Angell, according to SAAC's *Shelby Registry 1965–1967*. The car spent much of its life in Georgia with a swapped four-speed and a dual-quad Cobra induction system. In 2009 a subsequent owner, John Sparks, treated the Shelby to a rotisserie restoration, including a correct automatic transmission, prior to its sale to Daniel. Like many of the Hertz cars, Daniel's GT350H did not come with the over-the-top LeMans stripes, but they were added during the car's restoration.

Thanks to the Hertz program, Shelby American produced 2,378 GT350s in 1966, more than satisfying Ford's wish for increased sales—and profit—from the Shelby Mustang program.

5

1966 GT351 DRAG CAR

WHILE MOST OF THE MUSTANGS in this book are pristinely restored or well-preserved originals, that's not to imply that all Mustangs lived such a pampered life. Truthfully, many Mustangs from the 1960s served their useful purpose as daily drivers before being unceremoniously hauled off to junkyards or crushed as recycled metal. Only the lucky ones survived into the 1970s and 1980s, when enthusiasts began coveting them as collector cars, especially the fastbacks and convertibles. Today, performance models such as Shelbys, Bosses, and 428 Cobra Jet Mach 1s bring big dollars at collector-car auctions.

Often, used Mustangs were repurposed as race cars, bought from side yards and car lots as cheap yet racy-looking bodies for drag racing or oval track competition. In the south, Ford stock-car racers dropped Boss 302 small-blocks between the fenders to go head-to-head against Camaros on Saturday nights at the dirt tracks. Plentiful hardtops were frequently seen on quarter-mile drag strips with huge hood scoops and wide drag slicks, although the flimsy unibodies required extensive chassis stiffening to prevent the doors from flying open during speed shifts!

During the 1970s in San Antonio, Texas, a used-up Mustang was saved from the crusher when it was converted into a drag car. Since then, the 1965 fastback, now co-owned by Carl "Bernie" Bernstein and J. Bittle, has lived on drag strips from Texas to California, burning rubber a quarter- or eighth-mile at the time in 1966 Shelby GT350 livery. The car competed as a Super Pro bracket car in Texas and, later, Nostalgia C/Gas on the West Coast. Bernstein and J. Bittle currently campaign the Mustang in NHRA Super Gas and California's Nostalgic C/Gas, with both owners taking turns as driver.

"It's been a race car since the 1970s and evolved over time," explains J. Bittle. "A previous owner installed rear tubs during a 'back-half' upgrade in the 1970s. The lighter Mustang II front suspension was added in the 1980s, and for safety reasons I installed a tube chassis and four-link rear suspension after I bought it."

J. Bittle is proud of the fact that the car is not fiberglass bodied like many of today's door-slammer drag cars. "It's a real car," explains Bittle, who points out that the fastback body still carries its original sheet metal, although with a fiberglass front end. Not a real GT350, the fastback is painted in 1966 Shelby colors, Sapphire Blue with Wimbledon White "GT351" side stripes and over-the-top LeMans stripes. An R-model-type front valance aids cooling while a rear wing keeps the car stable at the top end.

Bittle's company, J. Bittle American (JBA) Racing, built the 393-cubic-inch stroker engine, starting with a four-bolt 351 Cleveland block and adding Ford Racing A-3 high-port aluminum cylinder heads, roller camshaft, and a 1,150 cfm Holley Dominator four-barrel on an aluminum intake. The combination makes 705 horsepower at 7,000 rpm on JBA's in-house chassis dynamometer, enough to propel the 2,300-pound fastback to 9.40-second quarter-mile elapsed times at 147 miles per hour. On the shorter eighth-mile tracks, the Mustang blasts to the finish line in 5.90 seconds at 115 mph.

Once just an old, used fastback, J. Bittle and Bernstein's GT351 Mustang continues to enjoy its second chance at life by competing at least once a month at the Auto Club Speedway in Fontana, Auto Club Raceway in Pomona, and the eighth-mile Barona Drag Strip in southern California.

6

1967 SHELBY GT350

AFTER TWO YEARS OF BUILDING souped-up Shelby Mustangs, Carroll Shelby recognized a sales trend. Instead of greasy T-shirt hot-rodders, the typical buyers for his GT350 were young professionals—doctors, lawyers, engineers—who craved image as much as performance and could afford to pay for it. They wanted a car that appeared different and sportier than the run-of-the-mill Mustang. Shelby gave it to them for 1967.

While the 1965–1966 Shelby GT350 basically looked like a Mustang fastback with scoops and stripes, Shelby took advantage of Ford's major 1967 Mustang overhaul to create a more distinctive look for his GT350 and new GT500. Making extensive use of fiberglass, the second-generation Shelby Mustang stood out with a 3-inch-longer front end with grille-mounted high-beam headlights and a dual-opening scoop on the extended hood. At the rear, a fiberglass trunk lid and quarter panel extensions formed an aggressive ducktail spoiler above distinctive wide taillights borrowed from the Cougar.

Continuing the upscale theme, the 1967 Shelbys came standard with the Mustang's aluminum-trimmed Deluxe interior, along with a unique woodgrain steering wheel and the first use of a roll bar with inertia-reel shoulder harnesses. Power steering and brakes were part of the fastback-only package.

Shelby American's 1967 advertising touted the new GT500 as powered by a dual-quad 428 Police Interceptor. The GT350 returned for a third year, however, with the same 306-horsepower version of the 289 High Performance small-block. Shelby American "Cobraized" the solid-lifter 289 with a Cobra high-rise aluminum intake manifold topped by a 715-cfm Holley four-barrel carburetor. Unlike in the 1965–1966 GT350s, tubular headers were not used. Instead, the cast-iron Hi-Po exhaust manifolds were retained. Finned aluminum Cobra valve covers topped off the Shelby engine.

Editor Jerry Titus compared the GT350 and GT500 for the March 1967 *Sports Car Graphic,* noting the handling difference between the small-block and big-block Shelbys: "The GT500 has a heavier feel," he reported. "The GT350 will go through the same corner appreciably faster and is less demanding from a control standpoint."

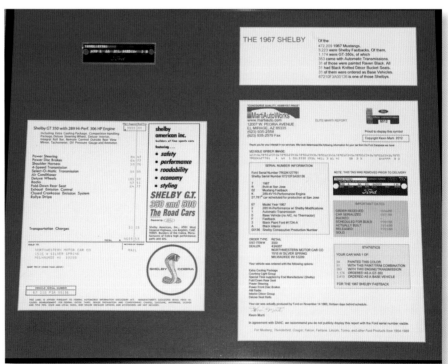

Kenny Worsham's rare black GT350 is considered one of the best 1967 Shelby survivors in existence. With just 26,000 miles, it still carries its original fiberglass, paint, interior, and spare tire. The combination of automatic transmission and production of only 54 in black implies that the car may have been ordered for a possible continuation of 1966's successful black-with-gold Hertz GT350 program. The Hertz contract was not renewed, however, and the black-with-white-stripes GT350 ended up at Northwestern Ford in Milwaukee, where the first owner drove it on sunny days only, accumulating just 18,000 miles over 10 years.

Numbered as 1967 Shelby 00136, Worsham's GT350 is equipped with several early production nuances, most notably the red "running lights" in the upper rear quarter scoops. Wired to come on with the brake lights and turn signals, the common freight trailer markers were initially part of the Shelby package, but were quickly discontinued when Shelby American learned they were illegal in some states.

In a similar manner, word also drifted back to Shelby American that a number of states outlawed the use of inboard headlights, which incidentally blocked airflow to the radiator, causing overheating issues in warmer climates. Grilles with outboard lights were hastily designed for cars destined for certain states. Today's collectors, though, prefer the sportier appearance of the inboard headlights, as found on Worsham's car.

Marketed as "The Road Car," the 1967 models transitioned the Shelby Mustang from the rough, racy earlier cars to the plusher models that followed. The 1967s were the last Shelby Mustangs built at Shelby American's Los Angeles facility. For 1968, the Shelby became less Shelby and more Ford as production moved to A. O. Smith near Dearborn.

7

1968 TRANS-AM COUPE

THE SILVER MUSTANG coupe roars down the front stretch, its Tunnel-Port 302 screaming at the top of its dual-quad lungs as driver/owner J. Bittle prepares to dive into Turn One with a herd of Mustangs, Camaros, and Barracudas on his tail. The sights and sounds are from the 1960s, but Bittle is living in the present-day world of Historic Motor Sports Association racing. For the speed shop owner from San Diego, mixing it up with the vintage competition takes him—and the race spectators—back to the glory days of Trans-Am.

In 1968, Ford engineer Ed Hinchliff bought a 1967 Mustang GT hardtop through the company's employee sales plan. Using his contacts at Kar Kraft, Ford's contracted racing arm, Hinchliff followed the factory formula to build his own 1968 Trans-Am Mustang. On July 4, 1968, Hinchliff drove his freshly built Sea Mist Green hardtop to a seventh-place finish in its inaugural race, the Paul Revere 250, a NASCAR Grand American event at Daytona Speedway. A month later he was mixing it up with Mark Donahue, Jerry Titus, Peter Revson, and the other top Trans-Am drivers of the day at Watkins Glen.

In the third year of Trans-Am, Mustang was the car to beat, having won back-to-back championships in 1966 and 1967. However, Chevrolet's new 302-powered Camaro Z/28, created specifically for Trans-Am, was making substantial gains under Penske Racing with driver Mark Donahue. For 1968, Ford confronted the small-block Chevy's horsepower advantage by bolting special heads onto the new 302-cubic-inch engine. Instead of restricting port shape and size to accommodate the pushrods, Ford engine engineers stole an idea from their NASCAR 427 and ran a pushrod tube directly through the huge, round intake ports, hence the "Tunnel-Port" name.

While the small-block Tunnel-Port engine made excellent power, especially at 7,000 rpms or higher, Ford made a tactical error by forcing the factory Shelby American team to use engines built by Ford engineers. The 1968 Trans-Am season was a Ford disaster; engine failures and the Penske/Donahue juggernaut combined to spoil Mustang's chance for a three-peat and handed the championship to Camaro.

It was into this Ford/Chevy battle that Hinchliff entered his new Trans-Am Mustang at Watkins Glen. He finished eighth in class and 13th overall, 21 laps behind winner Jerry Titus in one of only three Mustang victories in 1968.

For 1969, Hinchliff repainted his Mustang in Silver Mink and entered four major road races, including two Trans-Am events in which the privateer entry went up against the factory Boss 302s. The following winter, Hinchliff sold the hardtop to Steve Ross, who campaigned it in five Trans-Am races in 1970. Then, like so many used-up race cars, the Mustang was sold to a Mexican race team and faded into obscurity in the Mexico City FIA series.

As the popularity of vintage racing grew toward the end of the twentieth century, the Hinchliff/Ross 1968 Mustang was rediscovered and returned to the United States in 1995. The well-worn and battered old race car changed hands a number of times before J. Bittle acquired it to fulfill his desire to compete in historic races. Bittle returned the Mustang to its 1969 Hinchliff configuration, painted Silver Mink and powered by a rare 302 Tunnel-Port built by Bittle's company, JBA Racing. In the spirit of historic racing, much of the original car was retained, including the damaged floorpan that was crinkled in a 1969 Trans-Am race.

Since completing the restoration of the Hinchliff/Ross Trans-Am Mustang in 2002, J. Bittle has racked up numerous weekends on the track, including many southern California HMSA races and the Mustang 40th Anniversary Celebration at Nashville Speedway. Thanks to J. Bittle's former road-race warrior, the spirit of Trans-Am lives on.

8

1968
GT350 and GT500

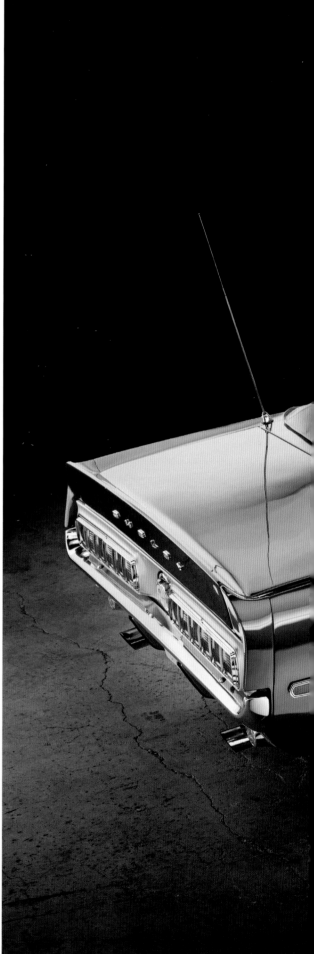

MUCH HAD CHANGED in the three years since Carroll Shelby introduced the first Shelby GT350, a loud and boisterous 1965 Mustang fastback that was often described as a "race car for the street." The following year, the sophomore 1966 GT350 was tamed for less race and more customer appeal with a quieter exhaust and added color choices. Year three saw the addition of a big-block GT500 model in a larger Mustang fastback with a Deluxe interior as standard equipment. Slowly but surely, the Shelby Mustang was moving away from its racing roots and evolving into a luxury GT, a revision that resulted in more Shelby sales for 1967 than the first two years combined.

The metamorphosis was complete when the 1968 Shelby arrived in Ford dealership showrooms. No longer powered by 1967's solid-lifter "Cobra" 289 and dual-quad 428, the updated GT350 and GT500 models got milder engines—a hydraulic-lifter 302 and a single four-barrel 428, respectively. The interior was Mustang Deluxe with woodgrain trim and a unique padded armrest for the console. Many 1968 Shelbys came through with tilt steering with power-assist, automatic transmission, and air conditioning, options not even considered for Shelbys just three years earlier. Mag-style wheel covers were standard equipment, with aluminum 10-spokes optional.

For the first time, a convertible joined the fastback in the Shelby lineup, further establishing the 1968 Shelby as a "Road Car." Like the fastback, the convertible was equipped with a roll bar, but it was finished in vinyl padding with a sculptured look. With the top down, the roll bar was a distinctive visual feature. Small rings provided an attachment point for owners to secure a surfboard.

The 1968 Shelby was more Ford and less Shelby, a reality supported by the fact that production moved from Shelby American in southern California to the A. O. Smith Company in Michigan. Carroll Shelby had lost his lease for the Shelby American buildings near the Los Angeles airport, and since Ford was more involved in Shelby Mustangs than ever before, it made sense to move the operation closer to Ford's headquarters in Dearborn. A. O. Smith had supplied fiberglass bodies for the Corvette in the early 1960s, so the company was experienced in fiberglass automotive panels, which were used extensively for the 1968 Shelby, including the hood, front nose, side scoops, trunk lid, and rear panel with 1965 Thunderbird sequential taillights. Ford shipped partially completed Mustangs to A. O. Smith's Ionia facility, where assembly line dollies rolled them through their metamorphosis into Shelbys.

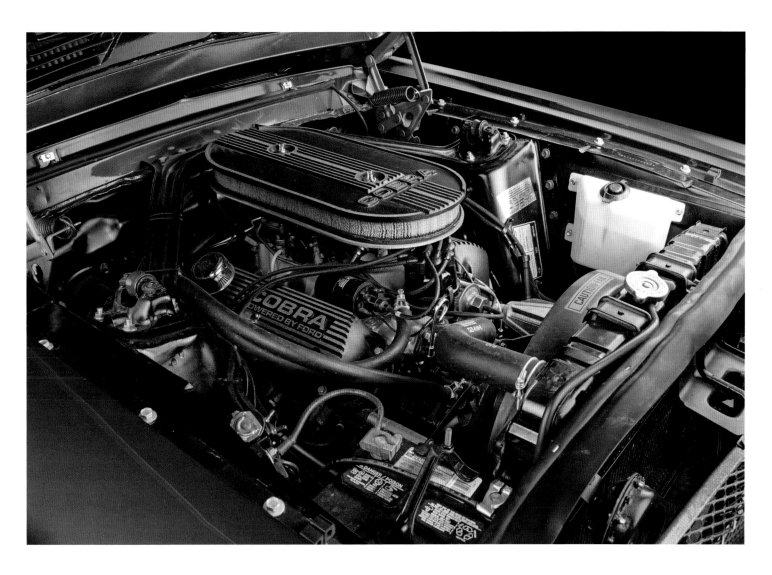

Although no longer packing rip-snorting powerplants for the racetrack, the 1968 Shelby engines were ideal for their new luxury GT objective. The GT350's 302-cubic-inch small-block was modified with a 600-cfm Holley carburetor on an aluminum intake for 250 horsepower, 20 more than the standard Mustang's optional four-barrel 302. For the GT500, a 428 Police Interceptor replaced the Mustang's 390 big-block, pumping out 360 horsepower with 410 cylinder heads, hydraulic-lifter cam, and Cobra aluminum intake with 715-cfm Holley four-barrel. For both the GT350's 302 and the GT500's 428, an oval "Cobra" air cleaner yielded the appearance of two carburetors underneath, like the 1967 Shelby's 428. However, a plate with two pins adapted the air cleaner lid to the single Holley carburetor.

Interestingly, some GT500s were delivered with 390 short-blocks, likely due to a Ford assembly line strike that interrupted the flow of parts. Owners were never told.

When Ford introduced the 428 Cobra Jet for the Mustang in April 1968, the new big-block replaced the 428 Police Interceptor and the GT500 was renamed GT500KR, for "King of the Road."

With lush Highland Green metallic paint and saddle interior, Ed Quinn's GT350 convertible is the quintessential luxury GT 1968 Shelby. When he retired from his job in the TV station business, Ed wanted a no-hassle Shelby to drive, so he targeted his search on 1968 GT350 convertibles. He found the right car in 2014 in Wisconsin: a freshly restored example with a four-speed and tilt-away steering column. Through the Marti Report, Ed learned that the Shelby had been originally sold at Northwestern Ford in Milwaukee, Ed's hometown. Thanks to the mild southern California weather, Ed puts the top down on his GT350 and gets out onto the San Diego roads at least once a month.

Frank Chirat is the third owner of his Sunlit Gold GT500 fastback, which was sold new by Gotham Ford in New York City before following its owner to California in 1969. Frank purchased the Shelby from Sunset Ford's used-car lot in 1981. "It had about 102,000 miles on it and was rust-free," Frank says. "Thankfully, most of the Shelby components were still there." Over the next 24 years, Frank added only 4,000 miles because, "It was worn out, smelly, and nasty!" In 2007 Frank completed a two-year restoration that retained as many of the original parts as possible. The day after picking up the Shelby from the restoration shop, Ed won first place and best of show awards at a Cobra Owners Association concours.

Carroll Shelby designed his COBRA GT to go like it looks

A brand-new Ford 302 cubic inch V-8 delivers for the GT 350. On the GT 500, a Ford 428 cubic inch V-8 is standard, with a new 427 V-8 powerhouse as a super-performance option. □ Four-speed transmissions are standard, close-coupled automatics are low-cost options. □ Great handling comes from competition-engineered suspension, 16-to-1 ratio power steering, adjustable shocks, heavy duty driveline and rear axle, and special high performance 130-MPH rated nylon tires. Front disc brakes, of course. □ And with this superb performance, Cobra GTs deliver head-turning styling *and* luxury, too. □ Interiors gleam with unique simulated wood grain trim on instrument panel, steering wheel, console and door panels. □ The exterior styling features *work* for you. □ Hood scoops supply extra carburetor air, fastback louvers are air extractors. □ Safety has not been overlooked — wide-rim wheels, integral overhead bar and shoulder harnesses are included. □ Carroll Shelby's unique fastbacks and new-for-'68 convertibles, are design-based on the Mustang, winner of two consecutive Trans-Am road racing championships. □ And that means real economy, a surprisingly low price for you. □ All four Cobra GTs say "Let's go!" □ See your Shelby Cobra dealer — and get going!

Shelby COBRA GT 350/500   POWER BY Ford

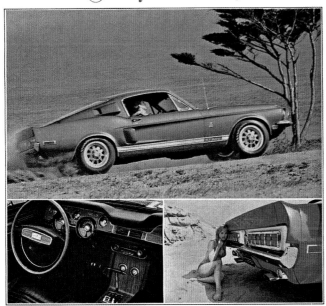

SHELBY COBRA GT 350/500
SPECIFICATIONS & FEATURES

All-new GT 350 and GT 500 convertibles feature integral overhead safety bar, many other performance, handling, safety and comfort features.

Get behind the wheel of a Shelby Cobra GT and you command a new motoring dimension. Carroll Shelby has worked a bit of racing car magic on the Ford Mustang. Result? The Shelby Cobra GT . . . a **true** road performer that rivals Europe's finest limited-production cars—but for thousands of dollars less. □ That's not all the news. Now you can own a Cobra GT 350 or GT 500 **convertible!** Same great features as the famed GT 350 and GT 500 fastback 2+2 coupes. □ If you love driving, you'll appreciate the pleasure of Cobra's thrilling GT performance and exclusive styling. It's a pleasure you can afford, as your Shelby Cobra dealer will gladly prove.

ENGINE SPECIFICATIONS

GT 350

Standard: All new OHV 302 cu. in. V-8; 250 horsepower @ 4800 rpm; 310 lbs./foot of torque @ 2800 rpm; 4.0″ x 3.0″ bore and stroke; compression ratio 10.5:1; hydraulic valve lifters. Cobra high velocity high volume intake manifold with 4 bbl carburetor with 600 CFM flow rate.

Optional*: Cobra centrifugal supercharger, 335 horsepower at 5200 rpm; 325 lbs./foot of torque @ 3200 rpm.†

NOTE: All Cobra GT engines include high velocity high flow intake manifolds, die-cast aluminum rocker covers, low restriction oval design diecast aluminum air cleaner, chromed filler caps, high capacity fuel pumps.

GT 500

Standard: All new Cobra OHV 428 cu. in. V-8; 360 horsepower @ 5400 rpm; 420 lbs./foot of torque @ 3200 rpm; 4.13″ x 3.984″ bore and stroke; compression ratio 10.5:1; hydraulic valve lifters. Cobra high velocity high volume intake manifold with advanced design, 4 bbl Holley carburetor with 600 CFM (flow rate) primaries, 715 CFM secondaries. High capacity fuel pump.

Optional*: All new Cobra hydraulic OHV 427 cu. in. V-8; 400 horsepower @ 5600 rpm; 460 lbs./foot of torque @ 3200 rpm; 4.235″ x 3.788″ bore and stroke; compression ratio 11.6:1; hydraulic valve lifters, advanced design cathedral float 4 bbl Holley carburetor. High capacity fuel pump.**

YOUR COBRA DEALER

KOONS FORD INC.
7 CORNERS
1051 East Broad St.
Falls Church Va.

The Desert Classic

	H	1968	SHELBY MUSTANG	GT500 COBRA
	Class	Year	Make	Model
	FRANK CHIRAT		MISSION VIEJO	CA
	Owner		City	State

This vehicle was sold new at Gotham Ford in New York City. One of two Shelby GT500's sold by Bill Kolb. The vehicle came to California in 1969 and retains the origional "Blue California License Plated" issued to cars coming into the state. I am the third owner. The previous owned had traded it in on a Ford Courier Pick up in 1981. I purchased it from Sunset Ford in Westminster. I worked for Ford Motor Company at the time as a Zone Service Manager and Sunset was one of my dealer accounts. It had about 102,000 miles on it and was rust free and most of the origional Shelby components were on it. For the next 24 years it was driven a total of about 4,000 miles, because it was worn out, smelly, nasty, and loud. In 2005 I made the decision to do a complete restoration which lasted 2 years. Weekly I would stop by the shop(s) and supervise, inspect, make changes, additions. I wanted to retain as many of the origional parts as possible, even if it had some patina. The first show the day after I picked it up at the shop it received a First Place 1968 Shelby and Best of Show at the Cobra Owners Concours. Shelby produced a total of 1,044 1969 GT 500's This vehicle has the 428 Police Interceptor engine. Special Shelby components such as a roll bar, shoulder harness, oil pressure and ampmeter guages, hubcaps, fiberglass hood, trunk and side scoops. Le Mans stripes and Marschal fog lamps. It has an 8-track/am radio, Hurst shifter and optional tilt-away steering wheel. Carroll Shelby has autographed the owner's manual and matching racing helmet. It has been shown on the lawn of the Playboy mansion, drag raced at California Speedway and driven to San Francisco since restoration.

9

1968-½
CJ FASTBACK

RHODE ISLAND FORD dealer Bob Tasca loved performance, but he wasn't happy with Ford's muscle car offerings during the mid-1960s. Tasca's competition boasted hot models including the Chevrolet Super Sport, Plymouth Road Runner, and Pontiac GTO. Ford had GT models with the 390, a torque monster for sure, but one that lacked horsepower when compared to Chevy's Turbo Jet 396 and Chrysler's Hemi. When *Hot Rod Magazine* paid a visit to Tasca Ford in 1967, the outspoken dealership owner spoke his mind.

"The 390 Mustang isn't competitive," Tasca told writer Eric Dahlquist while admitting that Ford claimed only 7.5 percent of the performance vehicle market in 1966. "That's shameful for a 'Total Performance' company."

Utilizing off-the-shelf pieces available from the Tasca Ford parts department, Tasca technicians built a hot 428 to replace the 390 in Bob Tasca's personal 1967 Mustang GT hardtop. *Hot Rod Magazine* reported 13.39-second quarter-mile times in its November 1967 issue. When the article landed on Ford president Lee Iacocca's desk, he wanted to know, "What are we going to do about the performance image problem?" Soon, Tasca was asked to deliver his Mustang KR-8—for "King of the Road 1968"—to Ford's experimental garage in Dearborn for teardown and inspection.

Just a few weeks later, in January 1968, four white Mustang fastbacks were unloaded at the NHRA Winternationals in Pomona, California. Powered by a new 428 inspired by Tasca's little street Mustang, they mowed down the competition, with driver Al Joniec marching through the field to win the Super Stock championship. Ford had a name for its new big-block—Cobra Jet, taking advantage of the Cobra name recently purchased from Carroll Shelby while also aiming a shot at Chevrolet's Turbo Jet nomenclature.

Hot Rod followed up with a second article in its March 1968 issue, describing the new 428 Cobra Jet Mustang as "the fastest running pure stock in the history of man," a quote that Ford snagged for its advertising campaign.

The publicity had Ford enthusiasts salivating for a street version. It arrived on April Fool's Day 1968 with the midyear introduction of the 428 Cobra Jet option for the Mustang GT and Fairlane, along with their Mercury siblings Cougar and Comet. Intentionally underrated at 335 horsepower for drag racing purposes, the CJ was basically a passenger-car 428 with Tasca's modifications—427-style cylinder heads, 390 GT camshaft, Holley 735-cfm four-barrel carburetor, and low-restriction exhaust manifolds. For the Mustang, the Cobra Jet was offered in conjunction with the GT option in all three body styles with either four-speed or C6 automatic transmission. A flat-black hood stripe and Ram-Air hood scoop, made functional with the use of a vacuum-operated flapper assembly on top of the air cleaner, set the CJ models apart from other GTs.

With its late introduction, Ford sold only 2,870 CJ Mustangs during the remaining four months of 1968 production—221 hardtops, 552 convertibles, and 2,097 fastbacks. But the 428 Cobra Jet quickly established a new performance image for the Mustang. Ford had even bigger plans for the Cobra Jet in 1969, marketing it with the new Mach 1 model topped by a Shaker hood scoop.

In the spring of 1968, Dan Stanley Ford's resident racer Dick Greak plopped down $3,800 for a white Cobra Jet fastback equipped with red interior and optional 3.91 gearing. For the next two years, Greak used his *Stanley Screamer* CJ as Ford intended—on the drag strip, blasting mid-13-second elapsed times to dominate Mo-Kan Dragway's D/Stock Automatic class in 1968 and 1969. Greak sold the Mustang in 1971, with third owner Jim Wicks overseeing a restoration to original in 2008 by Billups Classic Cars. Currently, the 11,200-mile fastback is owned by big-block collector Danny Laulom.

1969–1976

THE MUSCLE MUSTANGS

ON A WARM SUMMER EVENING in 1970, a Boss 302 Mustang rumbled through the parking lot at the Sugar 'n' Spice Drive-in, a popular gathering spot for teenagers and young adults in Spartanburg, South Carolina. The reflective side stripes glimmered under the street lights and the pulsing exhaust from Thrush side pipes—an owner add-on—tossed paper plates and Styrofoam cups out of the way as the Grabber Blue SportsRoof idled past the Falcons and Valiants parked under the awnings. The owner didn't need to rev the engine or spin the tires; everyone knew it was one of the baddest muscle cars in town.

The 1969 model year marked a turning point for the Mustang. After influential dealer Bob Tasca complained about Ford's insufficient performance offerings in a 1967 edition of *Hot Rod Magazine*, Ford president Lee Iacocca fired off a memo to his staff wanting to know, "What are we going to do about the performance image problem?" A few months later, the 428 Cobra Jet appeared in midyear 1968 Mustangs. For 1969, the CJ's street credibility jumped several notches when it was mated to the Mach 1, a new package for the Mustang SportsRoof that oozed image, especially when equipped with the optional Shaker hood scoop. And the Mach 1 was not alone. At midyear 1969, Ford introduced a pair of race-inspired models—the Boss 302, a Trans-Am car for the street, and the Boss 429, a Mustang fastback that homologated a 375-horse-power, hemi-head big-block for NASCAR racing.

With Torino Cobras and Cougar Eliminators added to the mix, Ford was suddenly on equal footing with General Motors and Chrysler in the muscle car wars.

But it was short-lived euphoria. Even as Boss 302 drivers Parnelli Jones and George Follmer were sipping champagne as 1970 Trans-Am champions, Ford and other manufacturers were facing increasingly stringent emissions and insurance regulations. In 1972, after a final year of performance excess with 1971 Boss 351s and 429 Cobra Jets, Ford pulled the plug on Mustang performance by lowering compression ratios and dropping big-blocks, focusing instead on luxury models like the Grande hardtop. When the OPEC oil embargo resulted in soaring fuel prices and long lines at the pumps, the smaller and fuel-efficient Mustang II was the right car at the right time. Ford attempted to recapture some of the old muscle car magic with Cobra II and King Cobra models, but the colorful stripes and graphics couldn't hide the fact that a two-barrel 302 was under the hood.

In just 10 years, from 1969 to the end of the Mustang II era in 1978, the Mustang went from muscle car darling to economy car. In today's collector car market, the high-performance 1969-1971 Mustangs bring top dollar at the big auctions while surviving Mustang IIs have a small but loyal following, especially for the Cobra IIs and King Cobras.

10

1969 BOSS 429

CHRYSLER HAD THE 426 HEMI; Ford was still competing with the side-oiler 427, a wedge-head engine that had been developed in the early 1960s. To continue its string of six consecutive NASCAR manufacturer championships dating back to 1963, Ford needed an updated engine in a hurry.

The engineers came up with the Boss 429.

Known inside Ford as the "Blue Crescent," the NASCAR-inspired Boss 429 was based on Ford's new "385" big-block engine family, except instead of the production 429's cast-iron canted-valve heads, it used specially-designed aluminum heads with huge ports and hemispherical-shaped combustion chambers, similar to Chrysler's Hemi. Ford chose to separate the two by identifying its combustion chambers as "crescent-shaped." The Boss 429 was one of the reasons why Chrysler's star driver, Richard Petty, jumped ship in 1969 to drive Ford's new Talladega, a fastback Torino with a 6-inch-longer nose and flush-mount grille to enhance aerodynamics on high-speed tracks like its namesake in Talladega, Alabama, the new 2.66-mile Alabama International Motor Speedway.

To meet NASCAR's homologation rules, Ford was required to sell 500 production versions of both the Boss 429 engine and blunt-nose Talladega. However, the NASCAR street cars did not have to be powered by the NASCAR engine. The Torino Talladega went on sale in early 1969 with the 428 Cobra Jet. To legalize its new racing engine, Ford chose to drop a street version of the Boss 429 into the 1969 Mustang SportsRoof.

But there was a problem: with its wide heads and valve covers, the Boss 429 would not fit into the Mustang's engine compartment. Because the needed modifications were deemed too complicated for Ford's Dearborn assembly line, final production was handed over to Kar Kraft, Ford's contracted performance operation. After acquiring a former mobile-home manufacturing plant in nearby Brighton, Kar Kraft set up an assembly line where partially completed 1969 Mach 1s could be converted into Boss 429s. The process involved reworking the inner fenders for an extra inch of clearance on each side before lowering the engine into place.

Compared to other muscle cars of the era, the Boss 429 Mustang was tame in appearance. Offered in five colors, the 1969 Boss 429 looked more like a base six-cylinder SportsRoof except for its 15-inch Magnum 500 wheels, chin spoiler, and large functional hood scoop. Identification was limited to small "Boss 429" decals on the front fenders, along with a "KK 429 NASCAR" number adjacent to each car's warranty plate underneath the latch mechanism on the driver's door.

Ford rated the Boss 429 at 375 horsepower, the most ever for a Mustang to date, but after detuning for the street with a milder camshaft and 735-cfm Holley carburetor, the race-bred powerplant lost much of its punch. But when modified with a high-lift cam and larger carburetor, the Boss 429 was capable of 11-second quarter-miles. The sight of a huge big-block under the hood frightened away most potential challengers anyway.

By producing 859 Boss 429 Mustangs for 1969, Ford more than satisfied NASCAR's homologation requirement. The Boss 429 Mustang returned for 1970, with 500 built in a wider variety of colors, including the popular Grabber shades.

Although the Boss 429 was not legal for NASCAR until mid-1969, the new engine, combined with the aerodynamic Torino Talladega (and its Mercury Cyclone Spoiler II sibling), served its purpose by helping Ford win the 1969 NASCAR manufacturer championship. David Pearson claimed the driver's championship by taking the checkered flag in 11 races with a Holman-Moody Talladega.

With their ultra-high performance NASCAR heritage, and low production numbers, the 1969–1970 Boss 429s today rank among the most coveted collector cars from the muscle car era. But that doesn't matter to San Diego's Marc Bodrie, who purchased his Black Jade 1969 Boss 429 from its second owner in 1986, just before values started to climb into the stratosphere. With less than 28,000 miles, KK 1351 remains in unrestored condition with the nonoriginal trunk spoiler and rear window louvers that Marc added many years ago.

Ford-Powered Double A Fuel Dragster.

Here's what happens when you put a 10.5:1 cr, 429 cid, V-8 in a Mustang...

Boss 429!

The cars in Ford's Performance Corner have to be winners. So we called all our competition engineers together and built a new road car—Boss 429.

We start with the same 429 block casting the NASCAR boys get. We four-bolt the mains, put in a forged steel crank, forged rods with ⅜ inch bolts, and forged pop-up pistons. She redlines at six and a half grand.

On top we went a little ape. Aluminum heads mated to the deck, huge canted valves that open way up on hydraulic lifters and forged rocker arms that just don't bend. Ports are oversized, chambers are crescent shaped. Manually controlled Ram-Air induction comes on strong via a 735 cfm 4-barrel Holley and aluminum high riser manifold. It all adds up to 375 horsepower, and that's understating it considerably.

We put the power on the ground through a 4-speed, heavy-duty box and a 3.9-to-1 Daytona type locker axle driving 7-inch chrome-styled-steel wheels carrying F60 x 15 Polyglas belted wide ones. The car stays where you point it with high-rate springs and shocks, plus heavy-duty roll bars fore and aft. Staggered shocks handle the torque problem. Power front discs do the stopping; power steering directs all the action.

What's the model? Thought you'd never ask! Mustang SportsRoof with dual racing mirrors, bright exhaust extensions, tach, front spoiler and full instrumentation. Another Going Thing. You'll find it at your Ford Dealer's Performance Corner. Or at the strip.

For your free copy of Ford's 1969 Performance Buyer's Digest, write: Performance Digest, Department HR, P.O. Box 1000, Dearborn, Michigan 48121.

MUSTANG *Ford*

11

1969 MACH 1 SCJ

BY LATE 1968, Ford was making strides in its marketing campaign aimed squarely at muscle car enthusiasts. Just a year earlier, influential Ford dealer Bob Tasca had publicly criticized Ford's stodgy image, complaining that 390 GTs were no match for 375-horse Chevy Super Sports and Pontiac GTOs. When the *Hot Rod* article found its way to Ford president Lee Iacocca's desk, he issued a memo to "fix Ford's performance image problem."

The 1969 Mach 1 was the first Mustang to fully address Iacocca's demand. Although its standard engine was a two-barrel 351, the new SportsRoof model oozed image with a blackout hood with racing-style click pins and scoop, side stripes, high-back bucket seats, and chrome styled steel wheels. Even the name implied "speed of sound." By the end of the model year, Ford had sold over 72,000 Mach 1s.

The Mach 1 was also the perfect platform for Ford's new 428 Cobra Jet engine, which had debuted midyear 1968 after Tasca had demonstrated his own KR-8 project, a 428-powered 1967 Mustang pumped up with components readily available over Ford dealership parts counters. For 1969, the 428 CJ was offered in two configurations: the standard Q-code or the R-code with a functional, air cleaner–mounted Shaker scoop that protruded through the hood and forced cooler outside air into the engine at wide-open throttle. Both were rated at 335 horsepower, a lowball number that may have been a ploy to bamboozle NHRA rule makers or a way to escape the wrath of insurance companies—or both. Some magazine reports estimated true horsepower at well over 400.

The 428 Cobra Jet was clearly aimed at a drag racing audience, both on the drag strip and, left unsaid, on the street. To take advantage of the CJ's tremendous torque and acceleration potential, Ford offered "digger" 3.91:1 and 4:.30:1 rear-gear options with Traction-Lok or Detroit Locker differentials. Realizing that customers who ordered the lower gearing would likely indulge in racing activities, legal or illegal, and to avoid costly warranty issues, Ford strengthened those 428 short-block internals with 427 LeMans connecting rods and cap screw bolts, which mandated different balancing for the crankshaft, flywheel/flexplate, and harmonic damper. Although the published power rating was not altered, the Q-code and R-code 428 engines in 3.91- and 4.30-geared Mustangs became known as "Super Cobra Jets."

Ford testing had also indicated that sustained higher engine speeds with the 3.91 or 4:30 gearing could cause overheating, so those cars were also equipped with an external oil cooler mounted on the radiator support.

Around February 1969, Ford started marketing the gearing, oil cooler, and stronger reciprocating package as the "Drag Pack," an option that continued into 1970 for Mustangs with the 428 Cobra Jet engine.

With an R-code 428 and the Drag Pack, Mark Tomei's 1969 Mach 1 is exactly what Ford had in mind with its marketing campaigns. Mark acquired the Mach 1 in the mid-1980s from the second owner, J. Bittle, who had helped maintain the car for its original owner. Bittle says he sold the SCJ Mach 1 in a "weak moment; it's one I should have kept."

In search of a replacement for the 1969 formal-roof CJ Torino that he had owned previously, Mark jumped at the chance to own the Acapulco Blue, white interior Mach 1 with the 428 Super Cobra Jet, Shaker scoop, four-speed, and Drag Pack 3.91 gears. It's the ultimate Mach 1, one that "will definitely throw you back into the seat," says Mark.

Mark bought the Mach 1 with less than 90,000 miles, and the odometer hasn't topped the 90,000-mile mark yet. "I've always had a four-door car for work," Mark says, "so I've pretty much stored the Mach 1 in my garage for the past seventeen years."

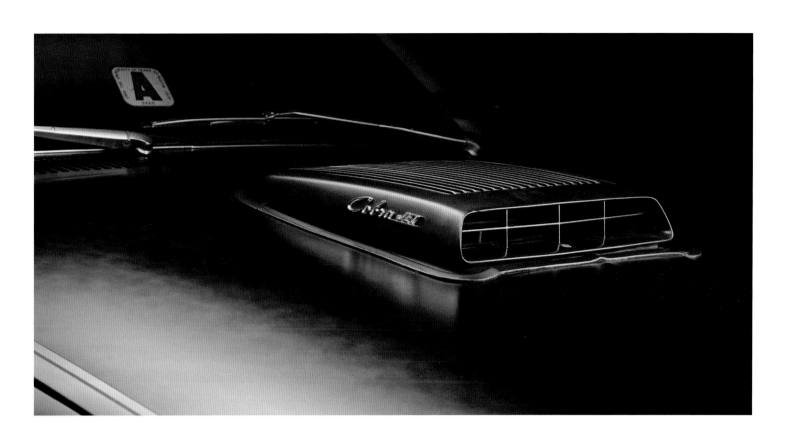

12

1970 BOSS 302 and BOSS 302 BARN FIND

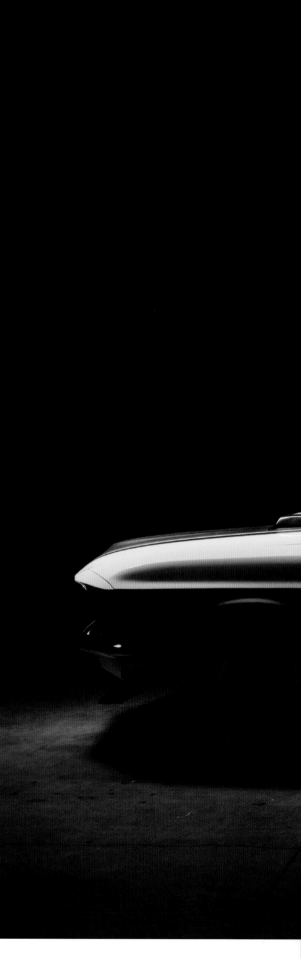

AS A YOUNG ENGINEER working his dream job in Ford's Engine Engineering department in 1968, Lee Morse recalls the moment when someone decided to bolt a set of prototype 351 Cleveland heads to a racing 302 short-block.

"The initial shot out of the barrel was very good," Morse said years later. "We obtained equal to or better performance than the 1968 Tunnel-Port, so we pursued it."

The Cleveland heads, with canted valves that allowed huge intake ports and valves, solved two problems for Ford. First, they worked better than the previous year's racing-only Tunnel-Port heads, which needed engine-destroying high rpms to make peak power. And two, they were scheduled for production in 1970, making them less expensive to produce, even though minor water jacket modifications were required to install them on the Windsor-style 302 block.

Less expense was required because Ford had bigger plans for the new engine. The Tunnel-Port 302 of 1968 never saw the inside of a production street Mustang, but for 1969, Ford needed to legalize the engine for Trans-Am racing and to compete with Chevrolet's Z/28 Camaro for street credibility.

Designer Larry Shinoda came up with the Boss moniker. "We wanted a name that would give it a special identity," Shinoda said in a 1981 interview. "Boss was chosen because it expressed the car's unique personality as a performance car. The name had charisma. It was also a handle our merchandising people could do something with."

The SportsRoof-only Boss 302 Mustang went on sale in April 1969 as a Trans-Am race car for the street. With a solid-lifter cam and 780-cfm Holley carburetor on an aluminum intake, the unique Cleveland-head small-block produced 290 horsepower, same as the Z/28. A four-speed manual was the only transmission choice, and air conditioning wasn't available. Due to its high-revving potential, an electronic rev-limiter protected Ford from warranty claims. Everything was heavy-duty, from the stout 9-inch rear axle mounted by staggered shocks to the extra bracing on the front shock towers to prevent stress fractures that could result from the grip by the massive F60x15 tires.

Topping off the 1969 Boss package was Shinoda's graphics package, consisting of reflective black side stripes, chin spoiler, and blackout treatment for the hood, headlight buckets, and rear panels. A pedestal-mount rear spoiler and radical rear window louvers were optional.

Mechanically, the Boss 302 continued into the 1970 model year with minor updates, including the addition of a rear sway bar and Hurst shifter. The external appearance was a different story, beginning with mildly redesigned sheet metal and two headlights instead of four.

'70 Boss 302—Son of Trans-Am.

The Mustang Boss 302 is what comes from winning Trans-Am races year after year. It's designed to go quick and hang tight. The standard specs sound like a $9,000 European sports job instead of a reasonably priced, reliable American pony car. Boss 302 comes in just one body style—the wind-splitting SportsRoof shape. The engine is Ford's high output 302 CID 4V V-8, with new cylinder heads to permit canting the valves for better gas flow and larger diameter. That's what gives you a big 290 horsepower from a small, lightweight 302 CID engine.

Choose either close or wide ratios on Boss 302's buttersmooth, fully synchronized 4-speed. We've made it an even quicker box by adding a T-Handle Hurst Shifter*.

Brakes are power boosted, ventilated floating-caliper front discs. When we tell you the sus-

pension is competition type with staggered rear shocks to combat rear wheel hop on takeoff, don't take our word for it, give it a try. We glue the Boss to the road on 15-inch wheels shod with F60-15 superwide fiberglass belted, bias ply tires. All this leaves you little to option but the fun things—like Magnum 500 chrome wheels, and those great Sport Slats for the tinted backlite. That's Boss 302. Your only problem . . . deciding whether to drive it or "Trans-Am" it.

For the full story on all the performance Fords for 1970, visit your Ford Dealer, and get our big 16-page 1970 Performance Digest. Or write to:

FORD PERFORMANCE DIGEST, Dept. CL-7,
P.O. Box 747, Dearborn, Michigan 48121.

MUSTANG Ford

Season after season Trans-Am wins with specially prepared Mustangs taught us how to set up Boss 302.

Paint a number on your Boss 302, put a big gas tank in it, and call yourself Parnelli Jones.

But it was Shinoda's stripe package that provided the 1970 Boss 302 with a look unlike any other muscle car on the road. The tape stripes ran the entire length of the car, starting at the leading edge of the hood before splitting off near the cowl and sweeping outward and over the fenders before sliding down the side of the car, with the "Boss 302" motif interrupting at the top. The hockey stick side stripes, made from reflective 3M material, flowed all the way to the rear bumper along the lower body line.

In 1969, Boss 302s were available in only four colors. But, for 1970, Ford opened up the palette to any Mustang color. The most popular was Bright Yellow, as found on 1,454 of the 7,014 Boss 302s produced for 1970, including the one currently owned by David Kelly, who in 2004 went on a search for a 1970 Boss 302 to park next to his 1967 Shelby GT500. "I liked the racing heritage and the fact that Ford only built them for two years," David explains. "I found this one on eBay and flew to Pennsylvania to see it. With only 43,000 miles, it was a very nice, clean car."

With the Boss back home in California, David initiated a two-year restoration, performing much of the work himself with assistance from Monroe Weathers at Mustangs West. Under one of the seats he discovered the assembly line build sheet, which allowed him to confirm the car's original equipment, including rear spoiler, rear window slats, Deluxe interior with console, tachometer, AM/8-track stereo, and 3.91 rear axle. During disassembly, David learned that his Boss is a numbers-matching car, right down to the carburetor, distributor, and VIN on the engine block, a rare find because most Boss engines were replaced under warranty due to a piston problem.

In contrast to David's low-mileage and immaculately restored Boss 302, Jordan Besenburch's Boss, also Bright Yellow, was pulled out of an avocado grove in 2014 after 27 years of neglect. David is the grandson of the original owner, who parked the Mustang under a tarp in 1988 after blowing up the engine during a street race. In tribute to his grandfather, David plans to refurbish the Boss, keeping the original paint patina but updating to a stroker 347-cubic-inch Boss engine built by JBA Racing.

13

1971 BOSS 351

IN NOVEMBER 1970, two months after the 1971 new-car introductions, Ford quietly slipped the Boss 351 into the Mustang lineup. No fanfare, no press preview, not even an ad in the major car magazines. The Boss 351 just suddenly appeared on dealer order forms, and only the wisest of performance enthusiasts were aware that the last, and arguably the best, of the Boss Mustangs had arrived on the scene for what would become the final year of the high-output, high-compression muscle car.

During the previous two years, Boss Mustangs had served the noble purpose of homologating their special engines for racing—the 302 for Trans-Am and the 429 for NASCAR. Both were compromised for pleasant street manners, with low-speed drivability suffering as a result. But when Ford pulled out of racing in the summer of 1970, there was no longer a need for legalizing engines with small displacement or Hemi heads.

Freed from restrictions, the Boss 351 put sufficient cubic inches underneath its large-port four-barrel Cleveland heads, essentially the same ones used on the earlier Boss 302. Based on Ford's new 351 Cleveland engine family, the Boss 351 matched the Camaro Z28's output by developing 330 horsepower, along with 370 lb-ft of torque, thanks to its solid-lifter camshaft, 11.0:1 compression, and 750-cfm Autolite four-barrel carburetor on an aluminum intake manifold.

Available only in the new-for-1971 Mustang SportsRoof, the Boss 351 was also equipped with mandatory high-performance goodies such as four-speed transmission with Hurst shifter, stout 9-inch rear end with 3.91 gears, Competition Suspension with staggered rear shocks, and functional Ram-Air through the new NACA-scooped hood. Externally, the Boss 351 was identified by its black or silver hood treatment, hockey-stick stripes, front spoiler, and small "Boss 351" decals on the front fenders and trunk lid. Magnum 500 wheels and a rear spoiler were popular options.

Ford
Official Licensed Product
5012

THE 1971 MUSTANG

Of the

149,682 **1971 Mustangs,**
60,453 were Sportsroofs. Of them,
1,806 were built with 351-4V Boss Engines. Of those,
344 were painted Grabber Yellow, of which
2 had Ginger Cloth Bucket Seats.
1 of these had Magnum 500 Chrome Wheels.
1F02R140586 is that Mustang.

Kevin Marti

For Mustang, Thunderbird, Cougar, Falcon, Fairlane, Lincoln, Torino, and other Ford Products from 1954-1989

In spite of its quiet introduction, the Boss 351 did not escape the attention of the car magazines of the day. *Sports Car Graphic* reported, "This thing goes like hell!" after clocking a 13.9-second quarter-mile elapsed time, a full second quicker than its Boss 302 predecessor. *Car & Driver* criticized the 1971 Mustang's increased bulk but described the Boss 351 as producing "generous power for its size and yet . . . remarkably tractable and docile."

Dan Ingebretson read the magazine reports while serving in the U.S. Air Force and requested a new Boss 351 from Keystone Ford in Norwalk, California, while he was stationed in Southeast Asia. "The dealer eventually located one at a dealership in Bishop, California," Dan recalls. "Someone had backed out of the deal, and the dealer was anxious to get rid of it. When I returned home, I delivered an F150 pickup to Bishop for the dealer exchange."

Dan has owned his Grabber Yellow 1971 Boss 351 ever since, initially using it as a family car while raising four children and even as a tow car for his dune buggy. After a repaint and engine rebuild in the 1990s, the Boss 351 was restricted to weekend duty, although Dan reports that he recently clicked off a 13.3-second pass on the quarter-mile at Fontana Raceway. Production data from Kevin Marti reveals that only two Boss 351s were produced with the Grabber Yellow exterior and Ginger Plaid interior color combination.

With ever-tightening government emission requirements, performance cars such as the Boss 351 Mustang were living on borrowed time in 1971. Ford was also out of racing, "which sort of leaves the Boss 351 dangling from the end of a limb that has been cut off," noted *Car & Driver*. For 1972, Ford joined the other auto manufacturers by reducing compression ratios and dropping high-performance engines, effectively ending the muscle car era.

The Boss 351 was the last rose of summer.

14

1972 GRANDE

THE 1972 MUSTANG showroom sales brochure described the Grande as "The ultimate in look, feel, and ride for sporty-luxury cars." Due to government regulations, performance models such as the Boss 351 and 429 Cobra Jet-powered Mach 1 had been discontinued, so Ford pointed its Mustang focus toward "Driving Machines" that offered luxury and style in a two-door pony car package. Driving home the point, the Grande was featured on four full pages in the brochure.

Three years earlier, the Grande had debuted as an entirely separate Mustang model, right alongside the new 1969 Mach 1. Offered as a hardtop only, the 1969 Grande packaged stylish Mustang options such as wire wheel covers and vinyl roof with unique appointments, including its own Deluxe interior and pinstripes. It was the first "personal-luxury" Mustang.

Even as the 1969 Grande arrived in dealer showrooms, Ford product planners were looking ahead to the Mustang's future. Foreseeing larger-displacement engines and unbridled performance potential, the Mustang for 1971–1973 grew 2 inches wider, 2 inches longer, and 600 pounds heavier than its 1969–1970 predecessor. The larger dimensions provided a more spacious interior for the driver and passengers, while a much-revised suspension added a comfortable Galaxie LTD-like ride quality. Unfortunately, the product planners were swinging at a curve ball as stricter insurance regulations and tighter government emissions standards conspired to curtail the predicted performance aspirations. So, when Ford shifted the Mustang's marketing objective from muscle to personal luxury, the larger 1971–1973 Grande turned out to be the right car at the right time.

The bright Grabber Blue paint and white top and interior on Jake Plumber's hardtop was an unusual color combination for the 1972 Grande. At a time when most Grandes were ordered in Ford's lush metallic colors, only 152 of the 18,045 Grandes built for 1972 were ordered in eye-catching Grabber Blue, according to Kevin Marti's Ford production database.

When Ford described the Grande as "standing alone at the top of its class," the statement was accurate because pony car competitors Camaro, Firebird, Challenger, and Barracuda did not offer a top-of-the-line luxury model. The Grande package for 1972 included color-keyed racing mirrors, chrome rocker panels and wheel lip moldings, pinstripes, vinyl roof, and unique wheel covers. Inside, the Grande stood out from base Mustangs with its own interior featuring high-back bucket seats with Lambeth cloth inserts, molded door panels with pull handles, rear ashtray, clock, and woodgrain trim.

That was just the start for Grande luxury. With the right options, the Mustang Grande approached Lincoln-like comfort and convenience. By checking off the right boxes on the order sheet, the Grande buyer could add SelectAire air conditioning, power side windows, AM/FM stereo with Stereosonic eight-track tape player, and power steering with five-way adjustable tilt column. The 250-cubic-inch inline six-cylinder was the standard Grande powerplant, but all Mustang engine options, right up to the four-barrel 351 Cleveland, were available.

As performance faded in the early 1970s, Grande sales increased each year from 1971 to 1973 era, with Ford producing nearly 61,000 over the three-year period. Alas, the Grande survived only five years; in 1974, the Mustang II luxury model was renamed "Ghia" for the Italian styling studio that assisted with styling for the new, smaller Mustang for the 1970s.

15

1976 COBRA II

LIKE MANY YOUNG MEN of the 1970s, Shawn McClure was mesmerized by the sight of blond bombshell Farrah Fawcett climbing into her 1976 Cobra II in the popular TV show *Charlie's Angels*. The image of the white-with-blue Mustang stuck with Shawn through the years, and 35 years later he began his search to acquire one just like it.

Oddly enough, it was Jim Wangers, best known for his marketing of the Pontiac GTO in the 1960s, who put some excitement into the Mustang II, which debuted in 1974 as a return to the Mustang's original proportions. In the early 1970s the Mustang had grown to intermediate size and Ford president Lee Iacocca, who originally conceived the idea of a four-seater sporty car in the early 1960s, wanted to return his pony car to its roots. Obviously, the Mustang for the 1970s needed to compete against Toyota Celicas and Datsun 240Zs, not Camaro Z/28s and Hemi 'Cudas.

Although John DeLorean, Russ Gee, and Bill Collins get the credit for dropping a 389-cubic-inch engine into the Pontiac Tempest to create the GTO, it was Wangers who built the mystique around America's original muscle car. Wangers promoted the GTO to the youth market by working with Ronnie and the Daytonas on the popular record *GTO* and also made a deal for the Monkees to drive a custom GTO on their TV show. Wangers' promotion of Pontiacs, which included the 1969 GTO Judge, transformed the General Motors division into one of the top American performance car companies of the 1960s.

But in the early 1970s, as Pontiac struggled to cope with increasingly stringent insurance and emissions regulations, Wangers left General Motors to form Motortown Corporation, a coach and accessories company that scored a juicy contract with Pontiac to build a Can-Am version of the LeMans. With the 1974 Mustang II in Ford showrooms, Wangers approached Edsel Ford II, then on Ford's board of directors, with a cosmetic concept for a Cobra II model in 1976. Eager to add some spice to the Mustang II's image, Edsel thought it was a great idea.

At a facility near Dearborn, Mustang IIs were converted into Cobra IIs with parts manufactured and installed by Motortown. The 1976 Cobra II recaptured some of the old Shelby magic with LeMans and rocker panel stripes, hood scoop, blackout grille with Cobra snake emblem, and ducktail rear spoiler. Even the available color combinations resembled the earlier Shelbys: blue with white, white with blue, and Hertz-like black with gold. For a touch of modernization, additional dress-up equipment included louvered panels over the quarter windows and, for the interior, brushed aluminum dash and door panel inserts.

The 13-inch wheels were either the Mustang II's standard silver-on-black Rallys or the optional slotted alloys, both with black "coiled snake" center caps for the Cobra II.

Conceived as a limited-edition model, the 1976 Cobra II surprised even Edsel Ford II by selling 25,259 units, no doubt aided by the exposure on *Charlie's Angels*. The model proved so popular that Ford moved production in-house for 1977 and 1978.

Shawn McClure admits that he was fascinated with the Cobra II that Fawcett's character, Jill Munroe, drove in *Charlie's Angels* and

initiated his quest to locate one in 2011. "I did an Internet search and immediately found one for sale," Shawn says. "It was the right color and in good condition." Shawn learned that the seller's grandmother had purchased the Cobra II new and drove it sparingly but never in the winter; it had only 32,000 miles on the odometer. "It was my lucky day," explains Shawn, who purchased the Mustang in its survivor condition and later equipped it with Mini-Lite-style four-lug wheels. Today, you'll find Shawn using his survivor Cobra II as a weekend driver around San Diego.

1984–2003

THE FOX-BODY MUSTANGS

WITH ITS MAJOR MAKEOVER for 1979, the Mustang lost much of its original character. Gone were the familiar design cues, including the wide-mouth grille opening, side sculpturing, and tri-lens taillights. Based on Ford's new Fox-body chassis, the 1979 Mustang took on a European flair, thanks to Ford design executive Jack Telnack, who had recently returned to Dearborn after a stint as vice-president of design for Ford of Europe. At first, the new Fox-body Mustangs were saddled with four-cylinder and small-displacement V-8s, down to 255 cubic inches. But a new performance era was on the horizon, one that would return the Mustang to the top of the American performance car scene.

The cover of the September 1981 *Motor Trend* said it all: "The Boss is Back—302 GT Mustang." With 157 horsepower, the new 5.0-liter High Output engine was the most powerful Mustang since 1973. It was certainly a step in the right direction and kick-started a new Mustang performance revolution. In 1983, the 5.0-liter gained a four-barrel carburetor for 175 horsepower. For 1985, a roller-lifter camshaft, tubular headers, and dual exhaust contributed to a 35 horsepower increase, up to 210. Electronic fuel injection debuted in 1986 with 200 horsepower, but a 1987 cylinder head upgrade boosted output to 225, where it would stay for the next five years.

Enthusiasts quickly jumped on the HO bandwagon. Powerful, lightweight, and inexpensive at around $12,500 for a brand-new 5.0-liter LX, the Fox-body Mustang became the drag racer's weapon of choice, especially after hot-rodders discovered that the EFI's EEC-IV computer was adaptable to modifications, including nitrous, supercharging, and turbocharging.

Soon, reports started filtering in from around the country about amazingly quick quarter-mile times by 5.0-liter pioneers. In early 1990, *Super Ford* magazine reported on three Mustangs using three different ways of making more power. In New York, "Stormin' Norman" Gray added a shot of nitrous oxide to turn 11.80-second quarter-miles. In Florida, Tom Hartsell installed a Paxton supercharger on his 1988 hatchback for 12.00 time slips. In Michigan, Ford engineer Brian Wolfe offered his 1986 GT as a test-bed for Ford SVO, running 11.60s in naturally aspirated form with experimental GT-40 heads and intake. The word was out. Soon, the staging lanes at America's drag strips were packed with street/strip 5.0-liter Mustangs, which spawned national racing series by Fun Ford Weekend and the National Mustang Racers Association.

While the 5.0-liter Mustang was enjoying newfound popularity in the early 1990s, inside the Ford hallways, executives were firing off interoffice communications about ditching the rear-wheel-drive Mustang in favor

of a front-wheel-drive chassis, all the better to battle the influx of sporty front-wheel-drive cars from Asia. When *AutoWeek* magazine leaked the plans, outcry from Mustang enthusiasts convinced Ford to rethink their strategy. A skunkworks operation, spearheaded by engineer/enthusiast John Coletti, resulted in an all-new Mustang, still based on the Fox-body chassis but with a body restyled to bring back many of the original Mustang's design cues. The front-wheel-drive project became the short-lived Probe.

It was a close call, one that eventually led to a revitalization of the Mustang brand. Ford's new Special Vehicle Team division polished the image with its Cobra model, which debuted in 1993, and, despite engineering setbacks, culminated with the most powerful Mustang to date—the supercharged, 390-horsepower 2003 Cobra that was code-named "Terminator." Along the way, Team Mustang's customization engineer, Scott Hoag, developed the 2001 Bullitt and 2003–2004 Mach 1 special editions.

16

1984 20th ANNIVERSARY GT350

TWENTY YEARS seemed like such a long time when Ford acknowledged the Mustang's 20th anniversary with a special limited-edition Mustang in the spring of 1984. Lyndon Johnson, the Beatles on Ed Sullivan, and 25-cent-per-gallon gasoline were all distant memories in the rearview mirror. In Ford showrooms, the Mustang celebrated its 20th birthday with a European-look hatchback or convertible with no resemblance to the sporty four-seater that had debuted on April 17, 1964.

In fact, Ford had even forgotten that it owned the first production Mustang, 100001, which had been stored in the basement of the Henry Ford Museum for nearly two decades. A 20th anniversary photo request from a car magazine tipped off Ford that the Wimbledon White 1964 1/2 convertible was sitting right under its corporate nose. Ford public affairs officials quickly pulled the historic Mustang out of its hiding place and posed it with the new 20th Anniversary Mustang for promotional photos.

"Recognizing this auspicious anniversary, Ford Motor Company is offering a Special Anniversary Limited Edition Mustang," announced the March 16, 1984, press release that accompanied the photo.

Arriving just in time for the Mustang's April 17 anniversary in both hatchback and convertible body styles, the 1984–½ 20th Anniversary Mustangs were decked out in Oxford White with Canyon Red cloth interior and red GT350 side stripes. The famous running horse tri-bar emblem returned to the front fenders, and a serialized plate with the owner's name was attached to the instrument panel. Based on the GT with a 5.0-liter V-8 or the Turbo GT with turbocharged 2.3-liter inline four-cylinder, the 20th Anniversary Mustang included the GT's front air dam with foglights, handling suspension with quad rear shocks, and rear spoiler.

Ford announced limited availability of 5,000 20th Anniversary models but actually produced 5,260, including 245 for Ford of Canada and 15 for Ford VIPs. According to the Mustang GT Registry, the majority were hatchbacks with the 175-horsepower (165 with automatic transmission) 5.0-liter V-8. Only 466 were equipped with the turbocharged four, rated at 145 horsepower and overshadowed by the intercooled and more powerful version in the top-of-the-line SVO.

At the time, a Ford public relations spokesman explained the GT350 stripes: "Since they were the first stripes used on a Mustang, we decided to use them on the 20th Anniversary car." Unfortunately, the GT350 in the side stripes sparked a lawsuit from Carroll Shelby, who originally conceived the name for his 1965 Shelby Mustang and still owned the copyright. It would take nearly 25 years to mend the resulting rift between Ford and Shelby.

San Diego's Marshall Corrie had two Mustang projects underway when he heard about a 20th Anniversary Mustang for sale, one of only 362 hatchbacks built with the four-cylinder turbo. "Because of the rarity, I stopped working on the other two cars so I could acquire it," Marshall notes. His anniversary car is equipped with the optional TRX wheels and Michelin metric tires, along with an also-rare dealer-installed sunroof. A previous owner added the reverse hood scoop, as used on the 1983 Mustang GT, and it remains on the car today

17

1986 SVO

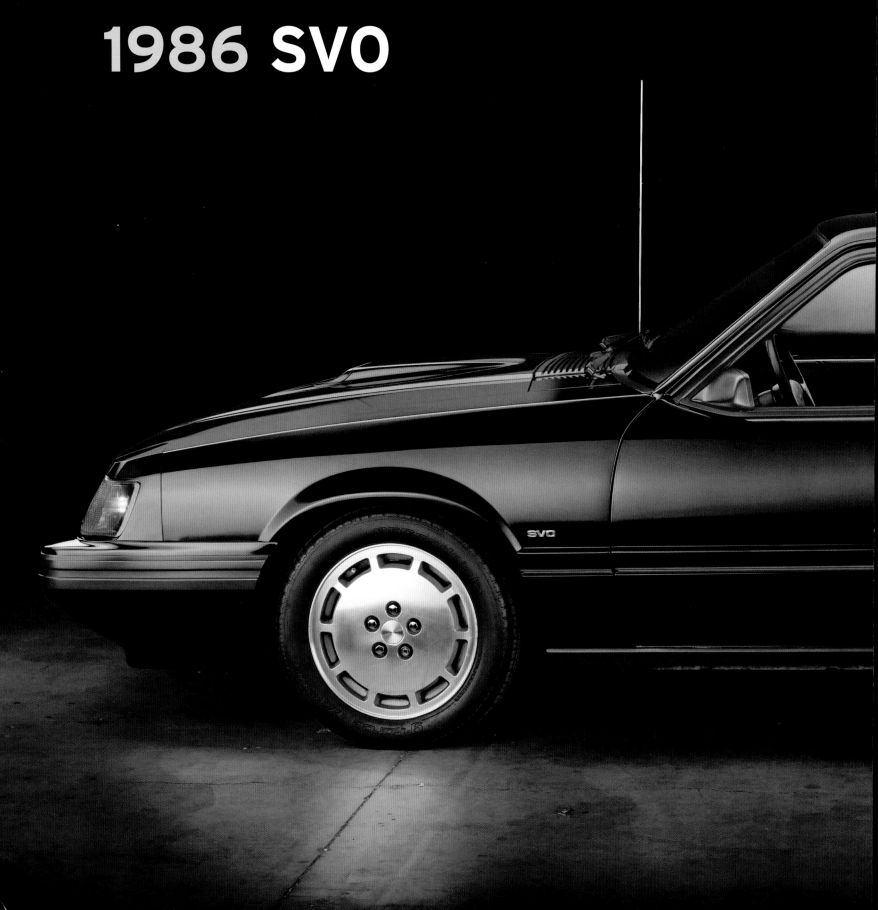

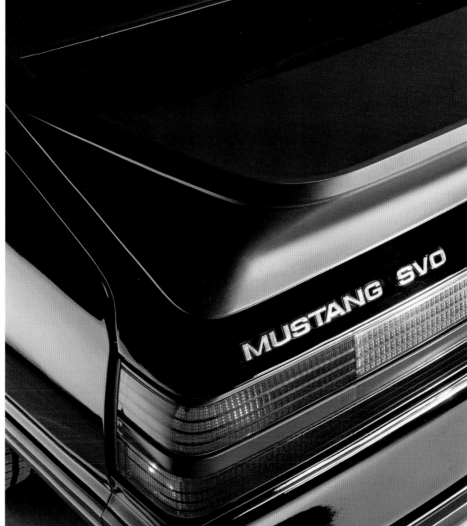

IN *MOTOR TREND'S* FIRST ROAD TEST of the SVO Mustang, writer Kevin Smith described Ford's latest pony car as, "Another milestone along the high-performance automobile's comeback trail."

It was 1983. After 10 boring years of emissions, fuel economy, and safety requirements, Ford was once again boasting performance with the introduction of the 1984 Mustang SVO, a model unlike any other in the Mustang's storied history. Ford described the sleek hatchback as a car "built by driving enthusiasts for driving enthusiasts." The new top-of-the-line SVO also marked the dawning of a new muscle car era, one that utilized technology instead of cubic inches to rank as one of the best all-around Mustangs ever made.

In September 1980, Ford had eased out of the 1970s' doldrums by announcing the formation of a new Special Vehicle Operations (SVO) group. Based on Ford of Europe's successful racing organization, a team of 30 engineers and designers, led by Ford of Europe's former director of motorsports Michael Kranefuss, was recruited and assigned three objectives: support private Ford racers, develop a performance parts program, and create high-performance production vehicles to help fund SVO's other activities. Unlike earlier Mustangs that competed against American competition like Camaro and Firebird, SVO aimed its Mustang squarely at import sports cars from Toyota, Datsun, and Isuzu. The game had changed.

The SVO came ready to play by tossing the Mustang's old V-8 playbook and starting over with a turbocharged 2.3-liter four-cylinder. Much improved over Ford's earlier turbocharging efforts, the Mustang's SVO package added an air-to-air intercooler with a functional hood scoop to generate 175 horsepower, same as the 5.0-liter V-8. But instead of torque, the SVO's punch came from the turbocharger's 14 psi of boost. To cope with emissions and CAFE fuel standards, Ford had embraced and fine-tuned its computerized engine technology, learning along the way that calibrations could also enhance performance. For example, with the SVO's new EEC-IV system, the driver could flip a switch on the instrument panel to change the engine parameters for regular or premium fuel.

The SVO established a number of other firsts for Mustang, including the first use of a floorboard dead pedal to brace the driver in hard turns, four-wheel disc brakes, 16-inch wheels, adjustable shocks, and a new Quadra Shock rear suspension, all of which would become standard equipment on future Mustangs. Externally, the SVO differed from lesser Mustangs with a sleeker nose, off-center hood scoop, and European-style biplane rear spoiler. As expected from an upscale model that stickered for $15,500, nearly $6,000 more than a 5.0-liter GT, the SVO's interior was substantially upgraded with perforated-hole cloth (or optional leather) bucket seats with adjustable lumbar support, 140-mph speedometer (at a time when 85 mph speedos were the norm), 8,000-rpm tachometer, unique trim, and Premium Sound.

The SVO continued into 1985 with few changes, including revised suspension settings and a switch from 3.45 to 3.73 gears. Later in the model year, the camshaft, exhaust, and other components were updated to increase horsepower to 205, along with other changes such as flush-mounted headlights. The improvements continued into 1986, the final year of the technologically sophisticated SVO. With the Mustang SVO's retirement, it went down in history as the only production car produced by Ford's SVO.

To ensure exclusivity, Mustang SVO production was purposely limited. Fewer than 10,000 were sold during the three-year production run according to the SVO Club of America: 4,507 for 1984, 1,515 for 1985, only 436 as the updated 1985 1/2, and 3,379 for 1986.

Bob and Brenda Radder acquired their black 1986 SVO in October 2005. Even with 155,000 miles, the interior remains all-original, although the body has been repainted. Like many SVO owners, the Radders have mildly modified the 2.3-liter engine, upgrading the turbocharger internals and adding an aftermarket blow-off valve, Boport camshaft, and 3-inch exhaust system.

18

1989 JBA DOMINATOR

TEN YEARS AFTER its debut as a 1979 model, the Fox-body Mustang was the hottest thing going on America's streets and drag strips. By the late 1980s Ford had perfected the production 5.0-liter High Output V-8 with EEC-IV electronic fuel injection and improved cylinder heads. Despite the early doomsday predictions about EFI, the 5.0 Mustang was ripe for modifying, with owners yanking out the inner fender silencer for improved intake airflow and torching off the original dual exhaust in favor of the cheap Flowmaster mufflers that provided the bellowing Mustang sound for a generation of owners.

Lightweight and inexpensive, the 5.0-liter Mustang spawned an entire industry of parts manufacturers, drag race series, and magazines. J. Bittle was right in the middle of the action.

Ironically, Bittle graduated from college in 1979, the first year of the Fox-body Mustang. His love of vintage Mustangs, especially big-block versions, led him right into the Fox-body explosion with the founding in 1985 of his J. Bittle American speed shop, where he pioneered the first smog-legal "shorty" header for the 5.0-liter Mustang. In the right place at the right time, by 1986 JBA was headquarters for Saleen Autosports High Performance Parts.

With his Saleen connection, Bittle ordered a new 1987 5.0-liter Mustang and had it converted into a Saleen R-model, which competed in a number of magazine shootouts. Later, Bittle used Saleen R029 to build JBA's original Dominator, a wide-body Mustang that Bittle described as "a Trans-Am car for the street." In 1989, when Ford supplied a 5.0-liter Mustang as a project car build for the Mustang's 25th anniversary, Bittle took advantage of the opportunity to expand his Dominator concept into one that was available to all Fox-body Mustang owners.

Dominator "B," as it became known, was the prototype for a fiberglass body kit available to all 5.0-liter Mustang owners through J. Bittle American. With wide fenders, 315/35ZR/17 Goodyear tires on 11-inch wide Monocoque wheels, and a roof-high rear wing, the JBA Dominator was a menacing sight on the southern California freeways where Bittle used it for daily transportation. Bittle made sure his Dominator lived up to its sinister appearance with a 450-horsepower, Vortech supercharged 5.0-liter V-8; Doug Nash five-speed with a Gear Vendors overdrive; and Wilwood brakes at both ends. In a February 1994 road test, *Motor Trend* described Bittle's Dominator as "wretched excess."

At the drag strip, the Dominator lived up to its name with a 12.2-second, 118.3-mph quarter-mile clocking, making it the quickest car in *Motor Trend*'s comparison test with other supercars of the day. On the skid pad, the big Goodyears paid off with a 1.09g measurement, a *Motor Trend* record at the time. "The Dominator is the most intense street Mustang we've ever encountered," the magazine said.

Motor Trend summed up the Dominator as "fast, noisy, socially irresponsible—and every teenage driver on the planet will challenge you to a race. The J. Bittle Performance Dominator may be just a big box of testosterone with wheels attached, but it's a thrill not to be missed."

JBA offered the turnkey Dominator package for $29,000, with available extras all the way up to twin turbochargers. For those not needing insanity, an entry-level package was offered for $10,000. Components could also be purchased separately for do-it-yourselfers.

Despite the car's domineering presence and performance credentials, JBA built only a dozen or so Dominators, making Bittle's Dominator B prototype one of the rarest and most significant Fox-bodies of all time.

19

1993 SVT COBRA

IN TERMS OF AUTOMOTIVE LIFESPANS, the Fox-body Mustang had a good run. Introduced in 1979, the third-generation Mustang, code-named FOX inside Ford, was redesigned from the ground up for a more European look and the integration of standard front disc brakes and a four-link rear suspension. For the first few years, the new-look Mustang struggled with the EPA's increasingly stringent fuel economy standards, resulting in a downsized 255-cubic-inch V-8 producing only 118 horsepower. But in 1982, everything changed when Ford announced that "The Boss is Back!" with the availability of a new 157-horsepower 5.0-liter High Output small-block. Over the next five years, the 5.0-liter evolved into a fuel-injected, 225-horsepower juggernaut that transformed the lightweight, inexpensive Fox-body Mustang into the top performance car of the late 1980s and early 1990s.

By the time Ford was ready to put the original Fox-body out to pasture after 1993, the platform and body had survived mostly unchanged for 14 years. A new Mustang, based on the Fox-body but significantly improved, was in development for 1994. But Ford had a surprise up its sleeve to send the original Fox-body out with a bang.

By 1990, Neil Ressler had spent 20 years climbing Ford's corporate ladder to reach the position of vice president of research and development. He was also a performance enthusiast and had supported Ford's SVO group in the 1980s. When the turbocharged SVO Mustang disappeared after 1986, Ressler felt there were still opportunities to enhance the performance of the 5.0-liter Mustang with help from an SVO-like program. He asked Special Vehicle Engineering designer Janine Bay to see if she could improve the performance of the Mustang GT.

Bay came back with a 265-horsepower prototype that benefitted from a revised suspension, larger brakes, and wider tires. With 40 more horsepower than the regular production 5.0-liter, Ressler considered calling it the Mustang GT-40, after the famous LeMans-winning Fords from the late 1960s. Then he learned that Ford would soon lose the rights to the Cobra name, purchased from Carroll Shelby in the 1960s but dormant since 1981. Ressler then instructed Bay, with help from another in-house performance enthusiast, John Plant, to put together a plan to produce a low-production, high-performance 1993 Mustang called the Cobra.

By shifting funds from his research and development budget, Ressler assembled a loose-knit gang of performance enthusiasts, all working outside their regular job duties at Ford, to develop the new Cobra. "We started calling ourselves the special vehicle team," Ressler said. Within a year, the group had become an official division within Ford known as SVT.

Arriving in Ford dealer showrooms in December 1992, SVT's Cobra lived up to its legendary name with 235 horsepower, 30 more than the 1993 GT thanks to Ford Motorsport GT-40 heads, unique intake manifold, and more aggressive camshaft. To support the extra power, four-wheel disc brakes, revamped suspension, and Goodyear Eagle P245/45ZR17 tires were added to the package. Visually, the Cobra differed from the GT with a narrow grille opening with small running horse emblem, rear spoiler, white-face gauges, Cobra snake emblems on the fenders, vane-style 17-inch aluminum wheels, and exterior color choices of Vibrant Red, Teal Metallic, or Black.

Later in 1993, SVT introduced the Cobra R, a turnkey competition version with deleted rear seat, air conditioning, and radio, along with adjustable struts/shocks and larger brakes.

Cobra production was limited on purpose; only 5,100 were built, including 107 Cobra Rs. But SVT wasn't created to set sales records; it was designed to "polish the oval" with cars that showcased SVT's four hallmarks—Performance, Substance, Exclusivity, and Value. The mission was accomplished with the 1993 Cobra, which set the stage for future SVT Mustangs.

Vince Castrejon purchased his 1993 SVT Cobra in January 2010. Number 3434 out of the 4,993 built, the Vibrant Red hatchback remains all-original except for JBA nickel-plated headers. Even with 108,000 miles, most of them added by the first owner, the car still has its original paint. Vince uses his Cobra for car shows in the San Diego area.

20

1995 COBRA "HARDTOP" CONVERTIBLE

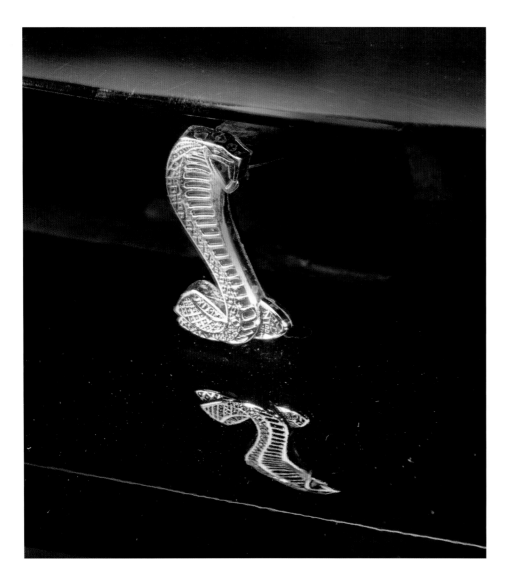

SOMETIMES, AT MUSTANG car shows, Jon Hoxter will park his black 1995 SVT Cobra with other SN-95 hardtops, then roll down the rear side windows. "Most of the owners walk right by, but a few will notice and ask how I did that," Jon says.

Jon's Mustang is one of only 499 Cobra convertibles delivered from the factory with a removable hardtop. And, like all Mustang convertibles, its rear quarter windows roll down, even with the hardtop in place. On regular hardtops, the rear windows are fixed.

Originally, Ford planned to offer the removable hardtop as an option for all 1994–1995 Mustang convertibles. But when the supplier had problems delivering the product, the $1,825 accessory was delayed until the 1995 model year and offered only for the top-of-the-line Cobra convertibles, all of them black with saddle interior and black tops, both soft and hard. Made from high-impact plastic, the hardtops were completely finished inside with a padded headliner and map light assembly, along with a unique wiring harness feeding power to the interior light and rear window defogger. Plugging in the wiring pigtail defeated the convertible top operation.

The hardtop attached to the convertible body with five latches, two at the front and three at the rear, with a two-piece interior package tray included to hide the retracted soft convertible top when the hardtop was in place. Weighing 90 pounds, installation and removal was a two-man job. Ford conveniently provided a rolling stand, which held the top upright, for storage.

Because the windshield header and rear attachment points were unique, the hardtop could not be secured to a regular production 1994–1995 Mustang convertible.

The 1995 Cobra was the final hurrah for the Windsor-style pushrod V-8, which had been used under Mustang hoods since the pony car's introduction in 1964. Based on the 215-horsepower 5.0-liter High Output, the 1994–1995 Cobra small-block received a 25-horsepower boost—up to 240—thanks to GT-40 cylinder heads, Crane roller-rocker arms, and free-flowing GT-40 intake manifold. Not surprisingly, the performance-oriented Cobra came with the five-speed manual only. SVT also equipped the Cobra with larger brakes, leather-trimmed interior, and a "softer" suspension designed to work with the P255/45ZR17 Goodyear Eagle GS-C tires. Externally, the Cobra model differed from its GT brethren with round foglights in the front fascia, unique 17x8-inch cast-aluminum wheels, a more aggressive rear spoiler, and Cobra emblems on the front fenders.

Ford produced 4,005 Cobras for 1995 (not counting 250 special "R" models), including 1,003 convertibles, making Jon's hardtop-convertible a rarity among the rare.

Jon purchased his Cobra from the original owner, who revealed that he had purchased the car off the showroom floor at Swanson Ford in San Francisco. "The seller's Craigslist ad didn't say anything about the hardtop option," Jon notes. "When my wife and I arrived at his house, a number of other people were waiting to see the car, but since we were the first to call, we got the first right of refusal. We took it for a test drive and struck a deal to buy it that day."

To verify the Cobra's status as an original hardtop-convertible, Jon acquired a Certificate of Authenticity from Ford SVT. Now he can convince both car show patrons and judges that the hardtop was a true factory production option. "Some Mustang enthusiasts have heard about it," Jon adds, "but few have ever seen one in person."

As the owner of such a special and rare car, Jon strives to keep his Cobra stock using Ford NOS parts whenever maintenance is required. Appropriately, the only modification is the Cobra snake emblem in place of the factory Mustang running horse in the front grille opening.

21

2001 BULLITT GT

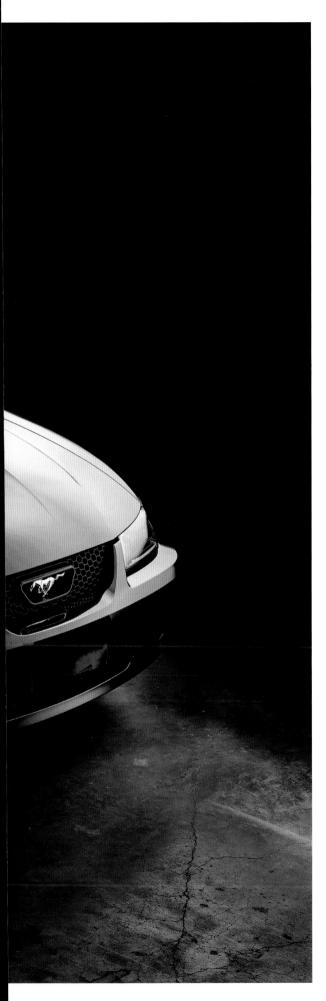

BY 2001, the Mustang was seven years into its FOX-4 makeover and three years into its latest New Edge styling update, with four years remaining before 2005's planned switch to a new platform. To spur interest in the dated body style, Ford's Team Mustang was looking for ideas for a specialty model when the answer dropped right into their laps. Team Mustang customization engineer Scott Hoag recalls how it happened:

While we were working on finding an appropriate feature car, the international auto show efforts were kicking in. Unbeknownst to me, Mustang design manager Sean Tant was asked to come up with a Mustang for the L.A. Auto Show and worked to deliver a Bullitt-themed coupe. He obviously knew that the 1968 Bullitt movie, with actor Steve McQueen in a 1968 Mustang fastback, had been popular. I was sitting in [chief program engineer] Art Hyde's office when we got the call from someone at the show saying, "All right, what's going on? We can't keep people away from this green Mustang." If there was that much excitement, then there was our feature car.

Although the movie *Bullitt* was not a commercial success in 1968, it became a cult favorite for its 12-minute chase scene involving McQueen in the Mustang, with the actor providing much of his own stunt driving, and the bad guys in a black 1968 Dodge Charger. Ford supplied two Mustangs for the chase, which leaped and bounced over the hills of San Francisco.

Team Mustang could have simply painted their special 2001 Mustang in Highland Green, like McQueen's fastback, but instead they took their Bullitt GT to the next level by elaborating on the vintage cues, adding 1960s-vintage instrument panel graphics and shifter ball, racing pedal covers, and brushed aluminum fuel filler cover. Even the C-pillar, quarter panel moldings, and rocker panels were modified for a more vintage vibe.

Even better, the $3,696 Bullitt package incorporated performance enhancements, starting with a 3/4-inch lower suspension with Tokico struts and shocks, special stabilizer bar, and subframe connectors. Brembo supplied the 13-inch front brake rotors with the first-time Mustang use of red calipers, which were readily visible through the five-spoke Bullitt wheels designed to look like the popular Torq-Thrusts rims from the 1960s. Under the scooped hood, the Bullitt GT 4.6-liter V-8 produced 10 more horsepower than the standard GT—up to 270— with a better-flowing aluminum intake manifold and twin-inlet throttle body, high-flow mufflers, and underdrive accessory pulleys.

Offered in Highland Green, True Blue, and Black, the 2001 Bullitt GT generated much-needed buzz for the FOX-4 Mustang in its waning years. When the car was introduced on January 4, 2001, Team Mustang announced a limited production of 6,500 cars, but only 5,582 made it into the pipeline by the end of 2001 production. Most were green like McQueen's 1968 movie car.

Bob Radder was a technician at San Diego's Bob Baker Ford when he witnessed the dealership's first 2001 Bullitt GTs rolling off the delivery hauler. "Two green ones and a black one," Bob recalls. "I fell in love with the package and had to have one."

There was only one catch. Bob already owned several Mustangs, and his wife of four years wasn't keen to add to the stable. She finally agreed, but with two demands—Bob had to make room by selling one of his other Mustangs and agree to start a family. "I sold my 1986 Mustang GT to my brother-in-law, and a few weeks later we found out my wife was pregnant."

Bob took delivery of his green Bullitt GT on May 7, 2001. The 3,000-mile Mustang remains 100-percent original, right down to the black label Motorcraft battery. "One son and one daughter later, we are still a Mustang family," says Bob.

22

2003 SVT COBRA CONVERTIBLE

SINCE ITS DEBUT IN 1993, Ford SVT's Cobra had been viewed as the Mustang's technology and performance leader. But during a desert road run for the proposed update for the upcoming 2002 model, SVT chief engineer John Coletti was clear in voicing his displeasure with the naturally aspirated 4.6-liter DOHC engine. At a fuel stop, Coletti told his team, "I'm going to go into this store and see if they sell Alpo. And I'm going to buy a six-pack and throw it into the back seat because this car is a dog!"

Coletti's scolding, which was immediately followed by what became known as the "picnic table review," sent the SVT team scurrying back to Dearborn with new marching orders. They made the drastic decision to delay the next Cobra, skipping the 2002 model year entirely, and went to work developing the first-ever factory supercharged Mustang. It would be worth the wait. With a Roots-type Eaton blower and water-to-air intercooler, the supercharged four-valve DOHC engine developed 390 horsepower and 390 lb-ft of torque to make the 2003 Cobra the most powerful Mustang ever offered by Ford. Inside the company, the project became known by its code-name—Terminator—a reference to Arnold Schwarzenegger's ferocious cyborg character in the 1984 movie of the same name.

With 70 more horsepower than the previous 2001 Cobra, the DOHC engine required significant strengthening, achieved mainly through Manley H-beam connecting rods and forged pistons. The aluminum heads were also revised for improved airflow. Previous Cobra DOHC engines had been built from regular production blocks assembled at Ford's Romeo engine plant, but the special nature of the 2003 version forced the first start-to-finish build on the Romeo niche line.

The Cobra's suspension, already lauded for its first use of IRS in a Mustang, was also upgraded, starting with more rubber on the pavement via 275/40ZR-17 Goodyear Eagle F1 performance tires on new 17x9-inch, five-spoke wheels. Other improvements included higher-rate springs all around, improved bushings, an additional crossbrace for the IRS, and monotube Bilstein dampers. To give the overhauled model a fresh look, the front end was redesigned with new foglight openings, a larger grille opening for cooling, and a lightweight composite hood with rear facing scoops.

Also for the first time, the convertible model received its own suspension tuning, an improvement that can be felt in Peter Arkin's menacing black 2003 Cobra. Arkin ordered it as

a 50th birthday present to himself in March 2002 and took delivery four months later, using it to replace his 1998 Cobra convertible, which he promptly passed down to his son. For the first year Arkin used the car as his daily driver, putting 20,000 miles on the odometer. Then, realizing the possible collectability factor of number 460 out of 5,082 Cobra convertibles built for 2003, Arkin "retired" the Cobra to weekend duty. Today, with 55,000 miles, the Cobra still has its original spark plugs and other maintenance items, except for tires and clutch. The radiator was replaced under warranty, and Arkin has enhanced the fun factor with K&N cold-air induction, Borla exhaust, and Steeda strut tower brace.

With its supercharged engine and independent rear suspension, the 2003 Cobra not only established a new performance standard for the Mustang, it also set a record for SVT Cobra sales, with 13,476 sold in both coupe and convertible body styles. "It handles like a slot car," says Arkin, who now drives his convertible mainly to car shows and cruises. "I never go to the gas station where it doesn't elicit comments from other customers."

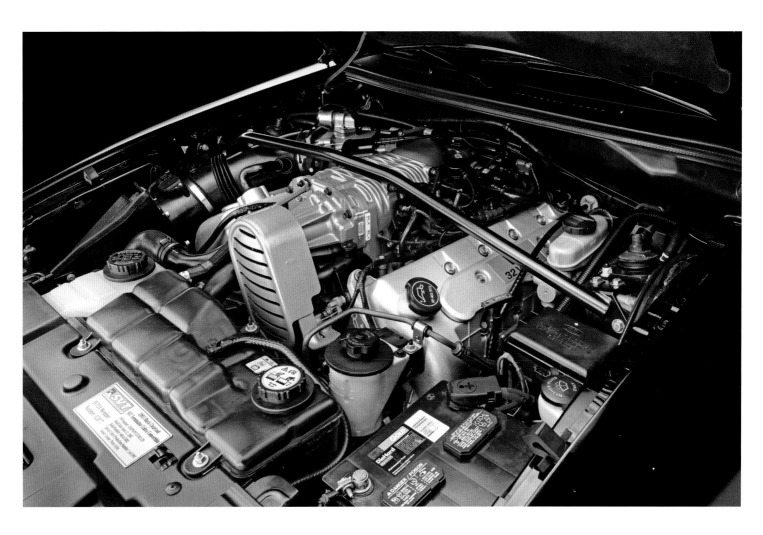

23

2003 MACH 1

EVEN BEFORE Team Mustang's 2001 Bullitt GT specialty model hit showrooms, customization engineer Scott Hoag was working on a proposal for a follow-up. He remembers the corporate reaction when he suggested bringing back the Mach 1 name for 2003: "The Bullitt had not been proven yet, and I was saying, 'Let's do another one! And we're going to put a hole through the hood!' They were thinking, 'We need a drug test from this guy. He's not right!'"

In the waning years of the Mustang's aging SN95 platform, Ford's Team Mustang began searching for ideas to maintain excitement and sales prior to the introduction of the all-new S197 model for 2005. Hoag and his boss, Mustang chief engineer Art Hyde, had conceived the Bullitt, a retro-styled coupe that honored the 1968 fastback driven by Steve McQueen in the 1968 movie *Bullitt*. It was a hit, especially among Mustang enthusiasts who appreciated the vintage vibe.

At Classic Design Concepts (CDC), owner George Huisman had found a marketing niche in providing 1960s-style aftermarket components—Shelby-like convertible light bars, sequential taillights, and side exhaust—to owners of late-model Mustangs. When CDC created a faithful reproduction of the 1969–1970 Mustang's Shaker hood scoop for the 1999 Mustang GT, Hoag took notice. The through-the-hood scoop, he realized, would make the perfect styling hook for the return of another Mustang muscle car name from the past.

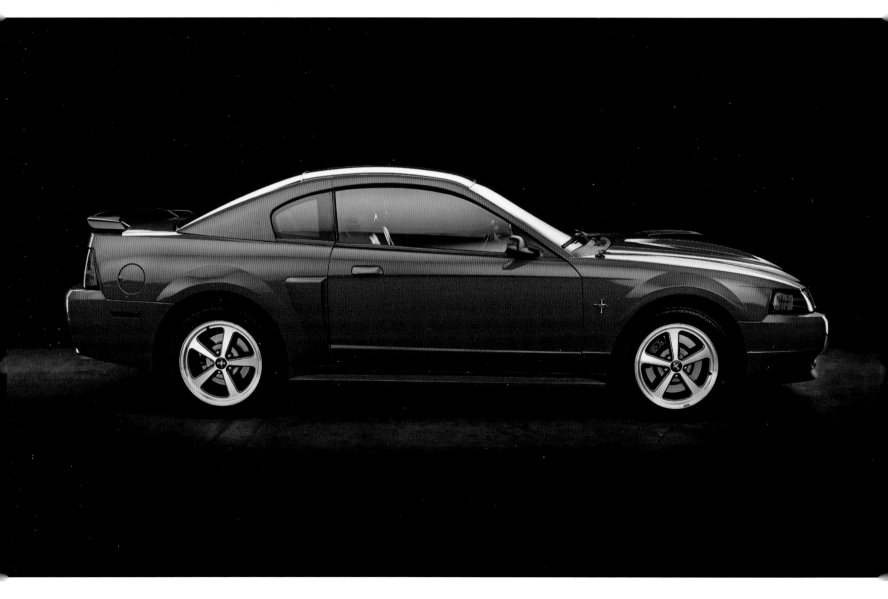

When quarter-mile testing proved that the functional Ram-Air also improved quarter-mile performance, the Shaker scoop became the focal point of a 2003 specialty model that honored the Mach 1 SportsRoof from 1969 and 1970. Other vintage styling cues included a black hood stripe on the domed hood, rear spoiler, retro-look instrument cluster and shifter ball, 1969-like Comfortweave high-back bucket seats, and rolled exhaust tips. To complete the "Total Throw-back, Complete Leap Forward" theme, the Mach 1 was equipped with 17-inch Heritage wheels designed to resemble the Magnum 500s from 1970. As an added touch, the exhaust was tuned for its own unique sound.

Like its Bullitt predecessor, the 2003 Mach 1 was more than a visual package. Since the 2003 Cobra's 4.6-liter dual overhead cam engine had been upgraded with a supercharger for 390 horsepower, Team Mustang brought back the 1999 Cobra's naturally aspirated DOHC 4.6, a high-revving, 305-horsepower powerplant that perfectly positioned the Mach 1 between the GT and the higher-priced SVT Cobra. On top was an exact duplicate of the 1969–1970 Shaker scoop with ducting underneath to funnel cooler outside air into the factory air cleaner assembly.

In magazine testing, the Mach 1 blasted through the quarter-mile in 13.8 seconds, about a second behind the Cobra that stickered for $5,000 more than the Mach's $29,000 base price.

Team Mustang offered the Mach 1 during the final two years of the SN95 Mustang, selling 9,652 for 2003 and 7,131 for 2004, according to the Mach 1 Registry. Only six colors were offered for 2003: Black, Dark Shadow Gray, Zinc Yellow, Azure Blue, Torch Red, and Oxford White, with Competition Orange added for 2004.

Today's Mustang collectors treasure the 2003–2004 Mach 1, but John Gerardy's 2003 Mach 1 is no museum piece. With 65,000 miles, the Torch Red coupe is still driven daily as a "company car" by Gerardy's son-in-law, Mike Vandewarker. It's great fun on the San Diego freeways thanks to a previous owner who had sent the Mach 1 to JBA Racing, where the original DOHC engine was rebuilt with custom pistons, then balanced and blueprinted for smooth, high-revving horsepower.

MUSTANGS

IN TERMS OF AUTOMOTIVE LIFESPANS, 25 years is an eternity. From 1979 to 2004, the Fox-body chassis served as the Mustang's underpinnings, taking the iconic ponycar from sporty economy car to 390-horsepower Cobra. But by the early 2000s, the much-upgraded Fox-body was showing its age. It was time for a change—and a challenge.

"When you're designing a new Mustang, you're the steward of forty years of automotive history," said Ford's J. Mays when describing the all-new 2005 Mustang. "If you don't get it right, you've got eight million Mustang fans to answer to!"

To bring the Mustang into the twenty-first century, Ford chose its modern DEW98 platform (basis for the new Lincoln LS) as the chassis of choice for the next ponycar. But by the time engineers were done modifying the platform for a sportier configuration, it had taken on the code-name S197. With a coil-over McPherson strut front suspension and a three-link solid rear axle with Panhard bar, the new chassis would serve the Mustang well for the next decade.

The first all-new Mustang in 25 years debuted for 2005 as a base V-6 and GT with a three-valve 4.6-liter V-8. While the chassis was all-new, externally, the design strategically maintained the Mustang's traditional long hood, short rear deck styling to appeal to baby boomers' nostalgic yearnings. The vintage look also provided opportunities to bring back iconic models from the past, like the California Special from 1968. In 2007, Ford SVT invited Carroll Shelby back into the Mustang fold by rebranding the Cobra as the Shelby GT500 with a supercharged 5.4-liter DOHC powerplant. A few years later, Team Mustang developed the most track-worthy street Mustang of all time, introducing it in 2011 as the modern iteration of the legendary Boss 302. Thanks to SVT, the S197 Mustang went out with a bang—the 2013–2014 Shelby GT500's 662 horsepower set a new output record for a factory-produced Mustang.

On April 17, 2015, exactly 50 years after the Mustang's introduction at the New York World's Fair, Ford Motor Company CEO Bill Ford introduced the 2015 Mustang 50th Limited Edition to the thousands of enthusiasts gathered in the Charlotte Motor Speedway grandstands to commemorate the Mustang's anniversary milestone. It was based on yet another total make-over, with the sixth generation finally incorporating an independent rear suspension to put the Mustang on par with its competitors. And for the first time, the Mustang was marketed as an international car, including right-hand drive from the factory for countries like England, Australia, and Japan.

For over 50 years, the Mustang has survived emission standards, oil embargoes, and even in-house efforts to switch to front-wheel drive. Thankfully, for over five decades the Mustang has remained true to its original purpose as a sporty, practical, and fun car.

24

2007 GT/CS

IN THE YEARS FOLLOWING the debut of the retro-styled 2005 Mustang, Ford reached back to the original pony car's heritage to market special models to the baby boomers who grew up with the iconic model in the 1960s. Two years into the S197, the GT/CS arrived at Ford dealerships to commemorate a special edition from 1968.

"California Made It Happen" was the slogan for the springtime promotion of the regional 1968 California Special Mustang. Unlike earlier special editions, the GT/CS went beyond special colors and packaged options by adopting the look of the popular Shelby Mustang with the use of a fiberglass rear spoiler, horizontal 1965 Thunderbird taillights, side scoops, and grille-mounted foglights. Marketed mainly in California but also sold in other western states and west Canada, the hardtop-only GT/CS sold in modest numbers, just 4,117. In recent years, however, the model's unique Shelby-like appearance has made it a collector favorite and show-stopping conversation piece.

Unlike the original from 1968, the 2007 GT/CS was available in both coupe and convertible body styles, and through Ford dealers nationwide, not just the West Coast. Primarily an appearance enhancement for the GT Premium Mustang, the California Special's $1,895 54C order code added a unique front fascia (with a larger grille opening that provided improved engine cooling and an integrated chin spoiler that lowered the front trim 1 1/2 inches), side scoops, black fadeout GT/CS tape stripes, bright rolled exhaust tips, California Special faux gas cap insert, and a unique rear air diffuser similar to the one on the Ford GT sports car. The Mustang GT's optional five-spoke, 18-inch polished aluminum wheels were also standard equipment. Initially, only four exterior colors were offered—Vista Blue, Performance White, Redfire, and Black—but additional colors, including Grabber Orange, were eventually added to the GT/CS palette. Inside, the GT/CS mandated the Mustang's Interior Upgrade Package, which provided black leather seats with either Dove (white) or Parchment inserts, GT/CS floor mats, and an array of bright polished and satin aluminum trim items. Many buyers also chose the optional GT Appearance Package, which added a hood scoop and engine cover for the 4.6-liter, three-valve V-8 powerplant.

As a side note, the GT/CS front fascia was designed with an eye toward use on a future Boss 302 model, which finally arrived in 2012. Both the GT/CS front fascia and the rear diffuser would be utilized for the 2006 Shelby GT-H and 2007–2008 Shelby GT programs.

By going national with the GT/CS program, Ford sold over twice as many in 2007 than in the original 1968 model year, producing 8,455 GT/CS Mustangs for 2007—5,885 coupes and 2,570 convertibles. According to Paul Newitt from the GT/CS Registry, nearly one in eight Mustang GTs produced in 2007 were California Specials. The GT/CS returned with minor updates for 2008 and 2009, then disappeared for 2010 before reemerging for the 2011–2014 model years.

California's Eric Benner is the original owner of his Redfire Metallic 2007 GT/CS convertible, a car that he calls *Aleanor* in tribute to his late grandparents, Al and Eleanor, who once owned a 1968 Mustang and passed down an inheritance that allowed Eric to purchase his Mustang brand-new in April 2007. At first, Eric used the GT/CS as his daily driver, adding enhancements such as a Ford Racing strut rod and rear blackout panel. But he soon retired his "special" Mustang to a more leisurely role as a weekend cruiser.

25

2008 SHELBY GT500

THE BEANS SPILLED when Carroll Shelby appeared with Ford brass at the 2005 New York Auto Show: Shelby and Ford SVT were teaming up to create a new Shelby GT500 Mustang. The bright red prototype, with iconic LeMans stripes over the roof, flexed its muscles onstage as Shelby and Ford group vice president Phil Martens shook hands over the vented hood. After an absence of nearly four decades, the Shelby name was back in a big way for Mustang.

Although rumors of a new relationship between Shelby and Ford had swirled around the halls of Ford World Headquarters for months, few expected the game changer that was revealed shortly after the introduction of the new-for-2005 S197 Mustang. Behind the scenes, Ford SVT had been working on its next Mustang Cobra, code-named Condor, with a supercharged 5.4-liter V-8. Leveraging a legendary name from Mustang's history, it became the Shelby GT500.

"Our goal was to build the most powerful, most capable Mustang ever," said SVT director Hau Thai-Tang. At first, SVT predicted 450 horsepower. But when the GT500 finally arrived in Ford dealer showrooms as a 2007 model, it boasted 500 horsepower from the supercharged 32-valve DOHC powerplant, a high-water mark for Mustang muscle.

SVT also described the GT500 as an "instant collectible," but it was much more than a museum piece as the engineers enhanced all-around performance with a Tremec TR6060 six-speed manual transmission, race-tuned suspension with GT500-specific Goodyear F1 Supercar tires, and Brembo brakes. Carroll Shelby served as a consultant during the development.

Externally, the new GT500 combined styling cues from both SVT and Shelby. The sinister-looking front end with prominent upper and lower grille openings was the main visual difference from the standard Mustang GT. Functional heat extractors in the raised hood dome allowed hot underhood air to escape. The GT500-unique rear fascia incorporated lower strakes inspired by the Ford GT supercar's rear air diffuser, and an add-on rear spoiler brought back a 1960s look. LeMans stripes were optional for coupes.

The Shelby look continued inside with special GT500 bucket seats and Cobra emblems, along with unique instrumentation that switched the speedometer and tachometer positions from their usual positions in the Mustang GT.

After the GT500 recorded a 12.7-second quarter-mile at 116 miles per hour, *Motor Trend* described it as a "fast, civilized, yet uniquely American grand touring coupe. No one in the world builds a car this charismatic, this accomplished, with this much performance, for the money. The greatest Mustang ever? No question."

Ford dealers sold 10,864 Shelby GT500s for 2007, making it the second-best-selling SVT Mustang ever, trailing only the 2003 Cobra. The special model continued mostly unchanged for 2008 and 2009, followed by cosmetic updates for 2010 and a dramatic horsepower increase to 662 for 2013 and 2014.

Southern Californian David Griffin had no intention of purchasing a new car when he visited Keystone Ford in Norwalk to pick up a F250 at the service department for his son's girlfriend. "While waiting, we were looking at new Mustang GTs," Dave says. "My son saw the 2008 Shelby GT500 sitting in the showroom and said, 'That would be a great car for you.'" At first, David balked at the dealer's $20,000 upcharge for the special SVT Mustang. Then the fleet manager came out and offered the black GT500 at sticker. "I told him to put a 'Sold' sign on it," David adds. "It was the first new car I ever bought. And I didn't even test drive it!"

David's Shelby is no garage queen; the 83,000 miles on the odometer were racked up during long-distance trips to Oregon, Nevada, New Mexico, Colorado, and Arizona. So far, the 72-year-old self-proclaimed hot rodder has resisted the urge to make modifications, noting that his GT500 is already "fast as hell" in its stock configuration.

26

2012 BOSS 302 LAGUNA SECA

BLACK WITH RED stripes and accents, it's hard to miss Bob Gardner's 2012 Boss 302 Laguna Seca as it rolls down the streets of Evergreen, Colorado. Of course, that was the reasoning for the contrasting colors on the track-prepped version of the modern Boss 302. Ford's Team Mustang wanted the car to be seen—and recognized—when it rounded the final turn, leading the pack.

Shortly after Ford introduced the 2005 Mustang with its retro styling, some within the company suggested moving forward with a modern iteration of the legendary 1969–1970 Boss 302, a SportsRoof Mustang created for Trans-Am racing. Others resisted, noting that it would be difficult to offer a credible Boss 302 with the 4.6-liter (281-cubic-inch) engine. So when Ford replaced the 4.6 with a new Coyote 5.0-liter (302 cubic inches) in 2011, the missing piece of the Boss puzzle fell into place. With Ford vice president of sales Jim Farley providing high-level support, Team Mustang decided to pursue the return of the Boss 302 as a purposeful performance car with road course capabilities. Mustang marketing manager Allison Revier described it as "a race car with a license plate."

Mustang chief engineer Dave Pericak understood that the engine was important to the Boss 302 heritage. Realizing that the 1969–1970 powerplant was a high-revving small-block, he quickly nixed the idea of supercharging and demanded a higher-output but naturally aspirated version of the new Coyote 5.0. By CNC machining the four-valve heads and adding a "runners-in-the-box" intake, Mike Harrison and his engine engineering team delivered 444 horsepower, a 32-horsepower increase over the 5.0-liter in the Mustang GT.

To make the new Boss 302 track worthy, Team Mustang equipped it with manually adjustable struts and shocks and Pirelli P Zero tires in staggered sizes—P255/40ZR-19 front and fatter 285/35ZR-19 rear. Expanding the Boss experience to the sound, NVH engineers Shawn Carney and Aaron Bresky devised a unique quad exhaust system with sidepipes that exited in front of the rear tires. Orifice plates with 5/16-inch openings maintained legal noise limits, but Carney and Bresky made sure the plates were easily removed for track days.

Introduced to the public in August 2010, the retro-striped 2012 Boss 302 drew rave reviews from the car magazines. *Motor Trend* called it "the best, most well-rounded Mustang ever." *Road & Track* raved: "The most agile Mustang we've ever tested."

But Team Mustang wasn't done. Concurrent with the regular production Boss 302, the engineers were also working on an ultimate track version. Named Laguna Seca to commemorate Parnelli Jones' first win of the 1970 Trans-Am season at the famous California track, the Boss 302 LS improved on the standard Boss 302's track worthiness with a chassis-stiffening X-brace in place of the rear seat, ducts for cooling the front disc brakes, a bolt-on scoop that cooled the transmission, a pedestal rear spoiler, a more aggressive front splitter, and Pirelli P Zero Corsa tires. The 2012 Boss 302 Laguna Seca was available in two colors, Black or Ingot Silver, both with contrasting red side stripes, roof, and trim.

In 2012, Bob Gardner resisted the urge to purchase a new Boss 302 Laguna Seca. But two years later, the bug bit again and he initiated the quest to find one with low mileage. An eBay ad turned up one in North Carolina with only 30 miles, so Bob flew out for a look. "It still had the plastic on the seats," he reports. "We struck a deal."

Today, Bob uses his black-with-red Boss 302 as a fun street car with occasional forays on the track at High Plains Raceway in Deer Trail, Colorado. "We have some great mountain roads around here too," he adds.

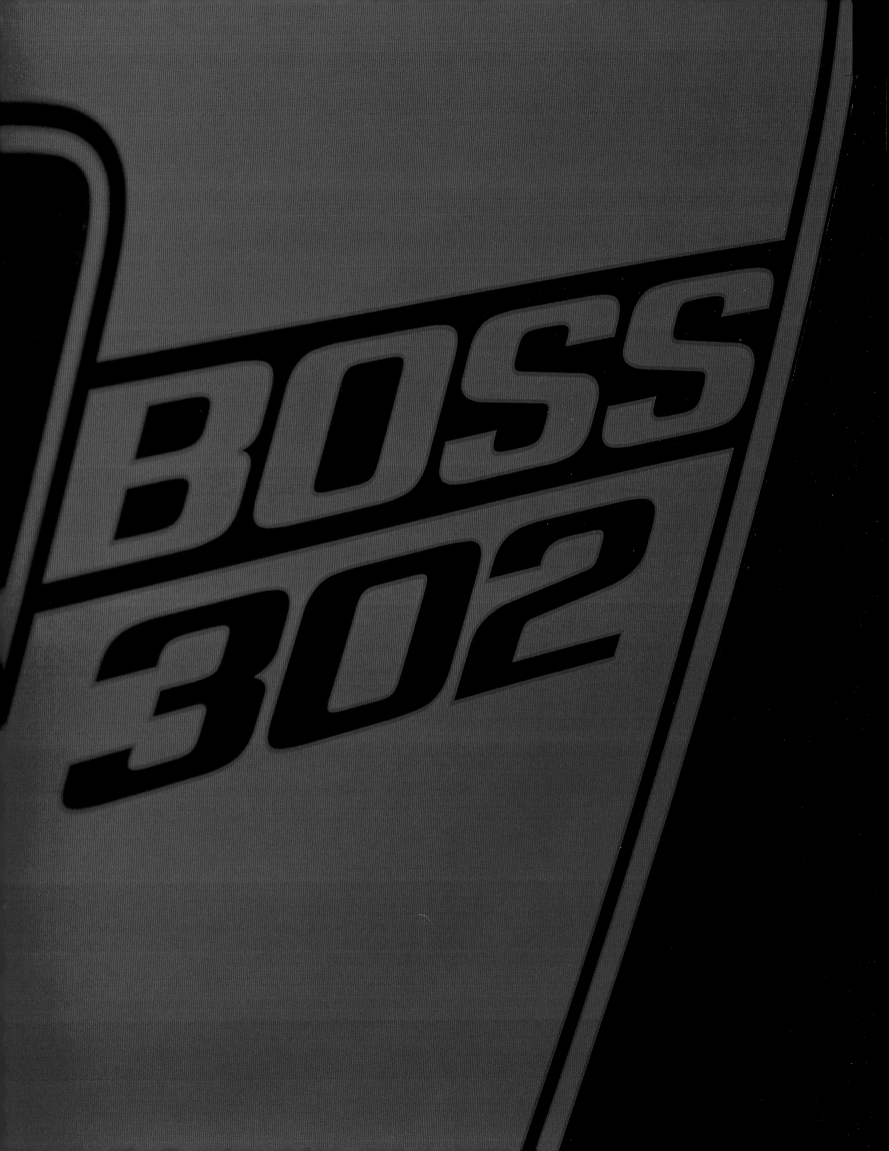

27

2014 COBRA JET

THE SCENE IN THE winner's circle was a flashback to the late 1960s. In January 2009, exactly 41 years to the month after Al Joniec's 1968 Cobra Jet Mustang won the Super Stock class at the 1968 NHRA Winternationals, a new iteration of the CJ returned to Pomona, California, and claimed a class championship again. Owned by Brent Hajek and driven by John Calvert, the white Mustang even carried the gold 1968 Rice-Holman graphics with Joniec's name on the roof in tribute. Ford Racing couldn't have written a better happy-ending script for its new competition-only Mustang.

The winning car was one of Ford Racing's new 2008 FR500CJ Mustangs, a factory-built car with a part number, M-FR500-CJ, and a new addition to the FR500 series of turnkey race cars. The Cobra Jet program proved so successful that it returned in limited numbers for the 2010, 2012, 2013, and 2014 model years. Loyd Swartz's white CJ is number 40 of the 50 built for 2014.

In 1968, Ford fired the shot heard throughout the muscle car world when it introduced the 428 Cobra Jet engine for the Mustang and other Fords. With 427-style heads, a Holley carburetor, and a GT390 cam, the big-block CJ finally gave Ford a street warrior to compete against SS Camaros and W-30 Oldsmobiles. To assist drag racers, Ford produced 50 special lightweight 1968 Mustang fastbacks with the new Cobra Jet engine.

For the modern Cobra Jet, Ford Racing followed a similar formula by offering only 50 FR500-CJ race cars each available year. Right from the factory, the Cobra Jet was ready for the track, right down to Goodyear slicks, a 9-inch rear end prepped by Strange Engineering, and NHRA-required safety equipment such as a SFI-spec bell housing and chrome-moly safety cage certified to 8.50-second elapsed times. Only minor prep and a skilled driver were required to turn it into a class-winning drag car. It even came with Recaro racing seats and available parachute mount.

Ford Racing started with a Mustang body in white, then packed it with the good stuff needed to go drag racing. The suspension was tailored for hard launches, including adjustability built into the rear three-link, Panhard bar, and competition struts and shocks. For hauling down the Mustang from speeds surpassing 150 miles per hour at the far end of the quarter-mile, Ford Racing bolted on a Strange Engineering brake kit featuring lightweight vented rotors and billet four-piston calipers.

Under the CJ hood, Ford Racing started with the production Coyote 5.0-liter short-block and modified it for competition with a forged crankshaft, Manley H-beam rods, and Mahle forged pistons. The factory four-valve heads were CNC-ported to take advantage of the custom grind camshafts and stainless headers. Two induction choices were offered: naturally aspirated with a Cobra Jet composite intake for an estimated 430 horsepower, or supercharged for well over 500 horsepower with Ford Racing's Whipple 2.9-liter blower.

For 2014, Ford Racing upgraded the transmission to a C3 automatic prepared by Joel's on Joy. Also, while earlier CJ cars were available only in white, Flat Black and the new Gotta-Have-It Green were added to the color choices, along with an optional Cobra graphics package.

Speaking of graphics, the "Super Cobra Jet" emblazoned across the hood of Swartz's 2014 FR500-CJ brings back yet another name from 1960s. Only this time, instead of a "Drag Pack" 428, the SCJ designates that the car is powered by the supercharged engine, which Ford advertised at 525 horsepower but the NHRA factored at a more-likely 543. Prepped by JBA Speed Shop in San Diego and driven by J. Bittle, the JBA-sponsored Mustang has run a best of 8.882 seconds at 153.32 miles per hour, making it one of the quickest 2014 CJ Mustangs in the country.

28

2014 SHELBY GT500

FROM THE OUTSIDE, the 2013 Shelby GT500 didn't look much different from the 2012 edition it replaced. There were some obvious tweaks, including a revised front grille treatment, new wheels, and quad exhaust tips peeking through the rear bumper cover. But it was what you couldn't see that made the difference in the next-generation GT500.

SVT chief engineer Jamal Hameedi joked that nearly every system in the 2013 GT500 had been upgraded "except for the back seat." That was an understatement, for under the power dome hood sat a brand-new supercharged and all-aluminum 5.8-liter (355-cubic-inch) V-8 in place of the previous year's 5.4. The combination of additional displacement and an increased-capacity Twin Vortices 2300 supercharger resulted in 662 horsepower, an impressive 112 more than 2012, and 631 lb-ft of gut-wrenching torque.

"The GT500 is the most powerful production car made in America and a fitting tribute to the late Carroll Shelby," proclaimed *Motor Trend* after blasting to an 11.6-second, 125.7-mile-per-hour quarter-mile clocked during a press day at Atlanta Dragway.

More than a straight-line bruiser, the new GT500 was equipped for world-class speeds. With revised six-speed gearing and long, lanky 3.31 rear axle, SVT estimated top speeds approaching, if not exceeding, 200 miles per hour. On the open road, the GT500's mild manners belied its explosive power. At 80 miles per hour, the engine loafed along at 1,600 rpm with little exhaust or road noise to interfere with the Shaker stereo system. The setup also benefitted fuel economy; with its 24-miles-per-gallon highway rating, the GT500 avoided the dreaded gas-guzzler tax.

Recognizing that horsepower generates heat, SVT focused on improving the GT500's cooling system by cross-drilling the block and heads for coolant flow, upgrading the fan, and adding a fan shroud with high-speed pressure-relief doors. They even eliminated the mesh inside the grille opening to make sure as much air as possible reached the radiator, especially at sustained high speeds. An optional Track Pack added an external oil cooler and pumps to cool the transmission and differential.

In addition to ranking as the most powerful Mustang of all time, the revamped GT500 was also technologically advanced. A 4.2-inch Productivity Screen, located between the 220-mph speedometer and tach, allowed the driver to flip through a number of options, including AdvanceTrac traction control, selectable steering, a variety of suspension settings, and Track Apps, which provided handy measurements for acceleration, g-forces, and braking. For fun with standing starts, a drag-strip Christmas tree popped up on the screen. Particularly impressive was Launch Control, designed to help drivers optimize quarter-mile times by providing preset launch rpms. Simply set the brake and mat the accelerator, then pop the clutch when the light hits green.

The 2013 Shelby GT500 continued into 2014 before cruising into the sunset when Ford introduced a totally new Mustang for 2015. As the final hurrah for the aging S197 platform, the GT500 established a new performance standard for Mustang. "Ford has improved its monster Mustang in every way possible," said *Motor Trend*, "with better handling, more technology, increased power, and even an improvement in highway fuel economy. This is truly the most potent pony car the Blue Oval has ever produced."

Adrian Garcia purchased his black-with-silver-stripes 2014 Shelby GT500 on Valentine's Day 2014, and it was love at first punch of the accelerator pedal. "It's my daily driver for work, and I show it on weekends," Adrian says. As if 662 horsepower from the factory wasn't enough, Adrian tweaked the output with a smaller supercharger pulley for more boost, a Steeda cold-air kit, JBA H-pipe, and SCT tune.

The 2013–2014 GT500 goes down in history as the last Shelby Mustang that Carroll Shelby contributed to at Ford. "I'm really proud to have my name on this car," Shelby told SVT engineers after a Sebring test session. "Working with my dreams, you guys have put together what I think a car should be. You've made it that and more."

29

2015 MUSTANG 50 YEAR LIMITED EDITION

AS THE LONGTIME OWNER of a vintage Mustang, Aaron Cardoza couldn't resist the opportunity to participate in a Military Overseas lottery that would give eight service members the chance to purchase a 2015 Mustang 50 Year Limited Edition. Hitting the jackpot, Aaron had his name picked, and in December 2013, while still deployed with the U.S. Army in Afghanistan, he placed his order for a Mustang that had not yet been introduced to the public. A year later, in December 2014, Aaron took delivery of his Kona Blue 50th anniversary car from Ford of Escondido in southern California.

"I wanted a Fortieth Anniversary Mustang back in 2004 but couldn't afford it at the time," Aaron says. "My wife told me I should just wait for the Fiftieth Anniversary model. So we had already planned to celebrate my twenty years in the army with the purchase of a 2015 Mustang."

With the 50 Year Limited Edition model, Aaron got more than just a 2015 Mustang, the latest and greatest pony car with a new S550 platform, restyled body, and independent rear suspension, a first for Mustang as standard equipment. Introduced by Ford Motor Company Executive Chairman Bill Ford during the Mustang 50th Birthday Celebration at Charlotte Motor Speedway, the 50 Year Limited Edition commemorated the Mustang's milestone golden anniversary with a special equipment package that recalled many of the iconic details from the original 1964 1/2 Mustang.

Based on the 2015 Mustang GT, the 2015 50 Year Limited Edition came loaded with options but only in two colors, Kona Blue or Wimbledon White, a shade similar to the first serialized 1964 1/2 convertible, 100001, which was purchased in April 1964 by Canadian airline pilot Captain Stanley Tucker. Powered by the Coyote 5.0-liter V-8 with 435 horsepower, the 50th package stood out with a number of styling cues, most notably the running horse corral and bars in the nose that simulated the 1965 grille treatment, along with the use of chrome on the side glass and taillights. Other special elements included a "50 Year" faux gas cap on the rear panel and louvered rear quarter windows made from layered sheets of glass, a construction technique developed specifically for the 50th Limited Edition.

Inside, the special model differed from other 2015 Mustangs with the use of an aluminum-trim panel with axel-spin finish, two-tone cashmere and black leather upholstery, and cashmere stitching for the seats, leather-wrapped steering wheel, instrument panel, and other interior components.

The 50 Year Limited Edition package also included the Performance Pack option with six-piston Brembo front brakes and 19-inch alloy wheels with Pirelli P Zero summer tires, making it the only 2015 Mustang available with both the Performance Pack and automatic transmission, one of the few available options for the 50 Year Limited Edition.

To commemorate the first year of Mustang production in 1964, only 1,964 Mustang 50 Year Limited Editions were produced, which created a mad scramble among Mustang enthusiasts and collectors to find one at Ford dealerships.

As one of the winners of the Military Overseas lottery, Aaron Cardoza didn't have that problem. His six-speed manual 50th anniversary car is number 513 of the 1,964. "I've liked Mustangs since I was a teen in high school," he explained. "My wife surprised me with my first Mustang, a 1965 hardtop, when I came home from training in 2003. Now I plan to keep both Mustangs, built fifty years apart, for many years."

ACKNOWLEDGMENTS

I WOULD LIKE TO THANK the many people who helped make this book so much better than I could have ever imagined. First of all, many thanks to my friend and mentor Randy Leffingwell for teaching me such a fantastic "light painting" photo technique. Longtime Shelby and Mustang owner/enthusiast J. Bittle, owner of JBA Speed Shop in San Diego, was an invaluable resource, helping me find many of the Mustangs for this book.

J. Bittle and his crew—Carl Bernstein, Austin Bittle, Stewart Bittle, Roger Cox, Mike Evans, Sean Kaschmitter, and Kurtis Stockton—also assisted on many late night photo shoots by positioning cars, wiping off dew, and even finding parts for some of the cars. Thanks as well to Rocky Frost from Custom Auto Body, and to the LA Shelby Club for getting the word out that I was looking for Mustangs. I am also indebted to Bartwood Construction and Aeroplex/Aerolease Group for finding some great photo shoot locations.

And of course, I couldn't have done it without the cooperation of the owners of the beautiful Mustangs: Peter Arkin, Eric Benner, Carl Bernstein, J. and Vicky Bittle, Marc Bodrie, Jordon Besenbruch, Aaron Cardoza, Vincent Castregon, Frank Chirat, Marshall Corrie, Adrian Garcia, Bob Gardner, John Gerardy, David "Pops" Griffin, Jon Hoxter, Dan Ingebretson, Bruce Kawaguchi, David Kelly, Danny Laulom, Shawn McClure, Jake Plumber, Bob and Brenda Radder, Ed Quinn, Loyd Swartz Racing, Paul Sequra, Dan Swana, Mark Tomei, and Ken Worsham.

This book is dedicated to Susan Loeser, my extremely supportive wife and best friend.

—Tom Loeser

IN 1980, automotive publishing entrepreneur Larry Dobbs took a chance by hiring a young, inexperienced Carolina country boy as the editor of *Mustang Monthly* magazine. I was only 28 at the time with a job resume that included elevator operator at a cotton mill and seven years of unloading fertilizer at my father's feed store—nothing that remotely prepared me for editorial responsibilities. But I had a passion for Mustangs, one that manifested itself by writing about Mustangs for club publications, then as a freelancer for *Mustang Monthly* before accepting Larry's job offer and settling in at a small magazine for what could have been a short-lived career.

As this book attests, I'm still writing about Ford's Mustang, an automotive icon that is loved around the world. For over 50 years, the Mustang has remained true to its roots as a fun, sporty, yet practical car. I've been fortunate to write about the Mustang—covering everything from its history to the owners who make the Mustang hobby and industry special—for nearly 40 of those 51 years.

Thanks, Larry, for the opportunity.

—Donald Farr

First published in 2015 by Motorbooks, an imprint of Quarto Publishing Group USA Inc., 400 First Avenue North, Suite 400, Minneapolis, MN 55401 USA

© 2015 Quarto Publishing Group USA Inc.
Text © 2015 Donald Farr
Photography © 2015 Tom Loeser

All photographs are from the photographer's collection unless noted otherwise.

Motorbooks titles are also available at discounts in bulk quantity for industrial or sales-promotional use. For details write to Special Sales Manager at Quarto Publishing Group USA Inc., 400 First Avenue North, Suite 400, Minneapolis, MN 55401 USA.

To find out more about our books,
visit us online at www.motorbooks.com.

ISBN: 978-0-7603-4786-7

Library of Congress Cataloging-in-Publication Data
Loeser, Tom, 1966-
  Art of the Mustang / Tom Loeser.
      pages cm
  ISBN 978-0-7603-4786-7 (hardbound)
  1. Mustang automobile--Design and construction--History--Chronology.
  2. Mustang automobile--Collectors and collecting.
  3. Antique and classic cars--United States. I. Title.
  TL215.M8L64 2015
  629.222'2--dc23
                                            2015018615

Acquisitions Editor: Darwin Holmstrom
Project Manager: Jordan Wiklund
Design Manager: James Kegley
Cover Designer: Simon Larkin
Layout Designer: Lorhill Design

On the front cover: The 1967 Shelby GT350.
On the back cover: The 1965 GT350 School Car
On the frontis: The familiar Mustang logo gleams from the grille of the 1965 model.
On the title page: The 1967 Shelby GT350.

Printed in China
10 9 8 7 6 5 4 3 2 1